IELTS STRATEGIES FOR STUDY

1 x TEXT BOOK
1 x CASSETTE

UPDATED EDITION

6/1/

IELTS: STRATEGIES FOR STUDY

IELTS

STRATEGIES
FOR STUDY

**READING, WRITING
LISTENING & SPEAKING
AT UNIVERSITY AND
COLLEGE**

Michael Garbutt & Kerry O'Sullivan

UPDATED
EDITION

National Centre for English Language Teaching and Research

IELTS: Strategies for Study
Updated edition

Published and distributed by the
National Centre for English
Language Teaching and Research
Macquarie University
Sydney NSW 2109

© Macquarie University 1991
Reprinted with corrections February 1995
Updated edition 1996
Reprinted 1998, 1999, 2000, 2002

National Library of Australia Cataloguing-in-Publication data
Garbutt, Michael D
IELTS strategies for study: reading, writing, listening and speaking at university
and college.

Updated ed.
ISBN 1 86408 182 1.

1. English Language – Examinations. 2. English Language – Textbooks for foreign
speakers. 3. International English Language Testing System. I. O'Sullivan Kerry, 1952.
II. National Centre for English Language Teaching and Research (Australia). III. Title.
IV. Title: International English Language Testing System strategies for study

428.34

The National Centre for English Language Teaching and Research (NCELTR) was
established at Macquarie University in 1988. The National Centre forms part of
the Linguistics and Psychology discipline at Macquarie University.

Printed by Ligare Pty Ltd, Riverwood NSW 2210
Cover design by Simon Leong Design

The authors take no responsibility for the factual accuracy of, or the views expressed in, reading passages in this book.

▶ CONTENTS

► ACKNOWLEDGEMENTS

We would like to thank the following people for their professional and personal support throughout the writing of this book:

Susan Benson	Stuart Holle
Jackie Bonham	Rohan Mead
Liz Campbell	David Nunan
Tan Teong Eng	Mavis O'Sullivan
Betty Garbutt	Martin Sitompul

We would also like to thank the students of the National Centre for English Language Teaching and Research, Macquarie University for their invaluable feedback. We are particularly grateful to:

Yuflinawati Away, Adiwar.

The tape accompanying this book could not have been made without the generous assistance of our colleagues:

Lynne Allen	Mark Gregory
Anne Burns	Liz Parkinson
Maree Delofski	Jenny Tindale
Helen Ferrara	Diana Simmons
Linda Gerot	Margaret Whetton

The authors gratefully acknowledge permission to publish an extract from the Macquarie University *Calendar 1991*, Business Law and Economics. They would also like to thank the New South Wales University Press for permission to include material drawn from *The Greenhouse Effect: Living in a warm Australia* by A. Henderson-Sellers and R. Blong.

Kerry O'Sullivan
Michael Garbutt
Macquarie University
Sydney

▶ INTRODUCTION ═══════

The purpose of this book is to help you focus on the English-language skills that you need in the IELTS test and the ways in which you can develop these skills.

▶ TEST DESCRIPTION

The IELTS test (the International English Language Testing System) assesses your level of skill in reading, writing, speaking and listening in English.

The test's four sections are administered in the following order:

- Listening — *40 minutes*
- Reading — *60 minutes*
- Writing — *60 minutes*
- Speaking — *11–14 minutes*

Each of the sections contains a variety of tasks designed to test your English-language proficiency. Although the range of tasks will vary from test to test, the strategies presented in this book are intended to develop a level of English-language proficiency which will enable you to deal with a wide range of different task types.

It is important to note that there are two different types of test. If you are planning to study at university you will be required to take the **IELTS Academic Module**. If you are planning to undertake a non-tertiary course or non-degree training you will be required to take the **IELTS General Training Module**. The format of both modules is identical but the reading passages and writing tasks in the General Training Module do not reflect tertiary study requirements. If you intend to take the General Training Module, you should pay particular attention to the General Training Module Sections on pages 8, 47, 54, 94 and 98, and in the *Practice Test Book* on page 45.

The **General Training Module** is designed for students who intend to enter non-tertiary or non-degree courses. The format of this module is identical to the Academic Module, but the reading passages and writing tasks do not reflect tertiary study requirements. General Training Module candidates take the same Listening and Speaking sections as other candidates. If you intend to take the General Training Module, you should pay particular attention to the General Training Module sections on pages 8, 47, 54, 94 and 98, and in the *Practice Test Book* on page 45.

The range of academic and professional fields in which candidates taking the IELTS Academic Module intend to study is, of course, very wide. You might be intending to study dentistry, or landscape architecture, mathematics, engineering, economics or literature. Whatever your intended field of study, you will take the same test as all candidates. As a result, the Academic Module does not require and does not test specialist knowledge.

The IELTS test does not assess

- general knowledge
- technical knowledge

The scores you achieve in the test will provide a description of your English-language proficiency. These scores will enable the institutions where you have applied to study to decide whether your English-language proficiency will enable you to perform successfully in tertiary study.

The IELTS test assesses

- your ability to read, write, listen and speak in the kinds of situations which are commonly encountered when living and studying in English-speaking countries.

Your basic aim, therefore, should be to become familiar with these kinds of situations and the language used in them.

Studying in English-speaking countries may involve

- reading books and journals
- writing assignments
- listening to lectures
- participating in tutorials and seminars

Reading books and journals

In tertiary study you need to be able to

- read a wide variety of recommended and other relevant books and journals
- find the information you require in texts, tables and diagrams
- critically evaluate what you read

In the IELTS Reading section you will have to read several passages which may be accompanied by tables and diagrams, understand the main points, locate specific information, and evaluate what you read.

Writing assignments

In tertiary study you may be required to

- analyse the set question or task
- read recommended and other relevant texts
- organise a writing plan
- write in your own words, showing that you have read widely

In the IELTS Writing section you need to analyse the question or task, organise a writing plan, develop an argument and then write it up.

Listening to lectures

In tertiary study you need to be able to

- understand rapid speech
- understand a variety of accents
- identify the main points
- take notes

In the IELTS Listening section you may be required to listen to a radio news item, for example one in which you hear native speakers using a range of accents. You need to be able to understand the main points and write them down.

Participating in tutorials and seminars

In tertiary study you need to be able to

- read recommended texts
- prepare to discuss the texts
- understand questions asked by the teacher and other students
- ask questions
- contribute to the discussion

In the IELTS Speaking section you will have to understand and respond to questions asked by the interviewer and ask questions yourself. For more details refer to the new IELTS Speaking Test insert.

Living in an English-speaking country may involve

- reading newspapers, notices, signs, instruction manuals, etc.
- writing to institutions and individuals
- listening to the radio, instructions, casual conversation, etc.
- speaking about yourself: your background, home country, study plans, etc.

These activities are relevant to all candidates, but are particularly important for General Training candidates, as they usually form the basis of reading passages and writing tasks in the General Training Module.

PREPARING FOR THE IELTS TEST AND TERTIARY STUDY

Your research

The tertiary study tasks listed above may not necessarily reflect the specific tasks you will be required to do, as these vary according to institution and discipline. You should contact the tertiary institutions that you are planning to study at and ask about the tasks you will have to carry out in the first semester or term. The following questions are designed to focus your research.

- Is there a pre-reading list?

- Can the institution supply you with a list of assignments from the coming year or previous years? How long are the written assignments expected to be?

- How is assessment carried out? Are there written exams, oral exams, practicals, continuous assessment or a combination of these methods?

- Will you be expected to give oral presentations? If so, can the institution supply examples of these tasks?

- How is formal teaching organised? Are there lectures? seminars? tutorials? laboratory work? field work? practical sessions?

This is a major research task which you need to begin before commencing tertiary study. In the IELTS test you are not expected to know the answers to these questions, but a knowledge of academic requirements will help you to focus your program of study for both the test and your future studies.

Your study program

You need to collect as many resources as possible.

You can use a *cassette recorder* to listen to pre-recorded materials, record radio and television programs, interview native speakers, and record your own speaking to analyse your performance.

You can use a *video recorder* in a similar way. In particular, a video recorder can help you to practise for the IELTS Speaking section.

Newspapers and magazines can help you to develop your grammar and vocabulary, to practise your reading strategies and to familiarise yourself with topics of general interest which may be relevant to the Reading, Writing and Speaking sections. A selection of useful newspapers and magazines is given on page 47.

As you work through this book and identify the language areas which you need to develop, you should build into your study program a selection of appropriate tasks from the wide range of English-language *textbooks* available. A list of relevant textbooks is given on pages 51, 93, 117 and 144.

Although bilingual dictionaries can be useful you should try to get used to using a *monolingual dictionary*, as this will extend your vocabulary and reading skills. A selection of monolingual dictionaries is given on page 51.

You should use *international radio guides* to select appropriate programs, such as interviews, news bulletins, documentaries and current affairs programs. If you are unable to obtain these guides from the consulates and cultural centres of English-speaking countries, you can write to the stations themselves.

You should also contact *cultural centres* of English-speaking countries, such as the British Council. These centres generally have extensive libraries, including books, newspapers, journals and video and audio tapes.

If possible, find a *study partner*. A regular arrangement to study with a partner can provide support, motivation and feedback.

Native speakers of English are also a valuable resource for practising speaking and listening, for getting feedback about your reading, writing and speaking, and for learning more about English-speaking cultures. If you do not know any native speakers, you should contact an English-speaking cultural centre and ask them for suggestions. They may have clubs and activity groups which you can join. You can also place an advertisement offering to teach your language in exchange for learning English.

Using this book

This book is designed to be used by all candidates for the IELTS test. It is assumed that you currently have at least an intermediate level of English-language proficiency.

IELTS: Strategies for Study contains four units: Reading, Writing, Listening and Speaking. The strategies presented in each unit relate to and reinforce each other. The units can therefore be studied in any order.

ANSWER KEYS

Tasks which have an answer key are marked with an asterisk, e.g. TASK 27*. Some tasks may have more than one answer. In these cases, the key provides some sample answers. If your answer is not included among these sample answers, you should check with your teacher or a native speaker of English.

This book is designed to help you identify your language needs and to provide a framework for your study program. The material is suitable for both independent study and classroom use. No recommended number of hours of study is given for the four units because individual learners will have different needs.

The passages presented in the book reflect the diversity of subject matter used in the IELTS test. As in the test itself, the subject matter of a particular passage may be unfamiliar to you. It is the use of appropriate strategies, not technical knowledge, that will enable you to find the information you require in these passages.

IELTS: STRATEGIES FOR STUDY

▶ UNIT 1 *Reading*

This unit contains

'I couldn't believe my eyes when I opened the test paper and saw that there was a passage about laser physics, with a really complicated diagram. I don't know anything about laser physics. I'm a systems engineer!

German IELTS candidate

'I ran out of time in the Reading section. The passages are too long.'

Thai IELTS candidate

▶ READING TEST DESCRIPTION

In the Reading Section, which lasts 60 minutes, candidates are required to read three passages and answer a total of about 40 questions. The passages, some of which may include diagrams, tables and pictures, range in length from approximately 300 to 1400 words in the Academic Module and from 20 to 1000 in the General Training Module. The test instructions indicate the amount of time you should spend answering each set of questions.

Because IELTS questions assess the kinds of reading skills required in tertiary study, a wide range of question types is possible. Although the precise format of the IELTS Reading section cannot be predicted, it is likely to contain:

- ◢ multiple-choice questions
- ◢ gap-filling exercises
- ◢ matching questions
- ◢ open questions

Examples of each type are given on pages 9, 10 and 11. This unit presents and practises a range of reading strategies relevant to all possible question types.

GENERAL TRAINING MODULE

Passages in the General Training Module are shorter and less linguistically complex than those in the Academic Module. Examples of General Training passages are presented in the *Practice Test Book* in Practice Test 4, on page 45. Note that the passages are less academic in style and content and reflect the kinds of passage you are likely to read in everyday life in an English- speaking country For example, passages could include:

- newspaper advertisements for accommodation
- cinema guides
- college timetables
- information about opening a bank account
- regulations regarding driving licences
- operating instructions for a compact disc player

Most of the passages in this unit are more academic in style and content than the ones you will find in the General Training Module and are therefore more linguistically demanding. The tasks, however, are designed to help you read more effectively and you should do them all, *paying particular attention to the strategies which are practised.*

ACADEMIC MODULE

What are the reading passages about?

The reading passages cover a very broad range of topics of general interest. They might include passages about education, technology, the environment or other contemporary issues. The important thing to remember is that you do not need any specialised background knowledge to read these passages and carry out the tasks successfully. Many candidates, such as the German systems engineer quoted earlier, believe it is impossible to answer questions about passages which deal with unfamiliar subjects. Remember that the test assesses your ability to use the effective reading strategies needed for any academic reading. Even though the passages may deal with subjects which you are not familiar with, you do not need any specialist knowledge to answer the questions. The test is not designed to assess your academic or professional knowledge of a particular subject.

SAMPLE READING TASKS

The five tasks presented below will familiarise you with the kinds of questions you may be required to answer in the Reading section of the IELTS test. In order to answer Sample Reading Tasks 1–5 you will need to re-read the Reading Test Description on pages 8 and 9.

SAMPLE READING TASK 1*: an example of a gap-filling task

The paragraph below summarises the section on this page called 'What are the reading passages about?' Five words or phrases have been left out. By referring to the section, find one or two words which fill the gaps. Write your answers in the column on the right.

Unfamiliarity with a ...1... may make candidates feel it is ...2... to answer the questions about the reading passages. It is important to note that the purpose of the test is not to ...3... technical knowledge but your ...4... to use the ...5... required for academic reading in general.

Write your answers here:

1. topic
2. impossible
3. ....
4. ....
5. ....

* With answer key

SAMPLE READING TASK 2*: an example of a gap-filling task

How long does the Reading section last? Write the appropriate letter in the space provided.

A. 300 minutes   C. 45 minutes

B. 60 minutes   D. 40 minutes

Your answer: 60

SAMPLE READING TASK 3*: an example of a multiple-choice task

What is the main point of the section entitled 'Academic Module'? Write the appropriate letter in the space provided.

A. Some candidates believe it is impossible to answer questions about passages which deal with unfamiliar subjects.

B. Many candidates are very concerned if they are unfamiliar with the subject of a reading passage.

C. The test assesses reading ability, not technical knowledge.

D. The subject matter is relevant to a candidate's area of study.

Your answer: C

SAMPLE READING TASK 4*: an example of an open-question task

The reading test description on page 8 refers to four kinds of questions and exercises. What are they? Write your answers in the space provided.

Your answers:

1. ....   3. ....

2. ....   4. ....

SAMPLE READING TASK 5*: an example of a matching task

Which of the following paragraphs (A, B or C) corresponds to the heading 'Question Types'? Write your answer in the space provided.

Paragraph A

In the Reading Section, which lasts 60 minutes, candidates are required to read

continued on page 11

SAMPLE READING TASK 5*: *continued from page 10*

three passages and answer a total of about 40 questions. The passages, some of which may include diagrams, tables and pictures, range in length from approximately 300 to 1400 words in the Academic Module and from 20 to 1000 in the General Training Module. The test instructions indicate the amount of time you should spend answering each set of questions.

Paragraph B
Because questions assess the kinds of language skills required in tertiary study, a wide range of question types is therefore possible. Although the precise format of the IELTS Reading section cannot be predicted, it is likely to contain ...

Paragraph C
Remember that the test assesses your ability to use the effective reading strategies needed for any academic reading. Even though the passages may concern technical subjects which you are not familiar with, you do not need any specialist knowledge to answer the questions. The test is not designed to assess your academic or professional knowledge of a particular subject.

Your answer: ....

▶ READING STRATEGIES

'The tutor handed out a photocopy and asked the class to read through it quickly so we could discuss it. Two minutes later she asked for comments. Some people had finished and I was still on the first paragraph.'

Hong Kong student of psychology at a British University

This student had difficulty because he did not understand the purpose of the task and therefore did not use appropriate reading strategies.

Before beginning to read any text – a book, a magazine or journal article, an IELTS reading passage – you should ask yourself three questions

- ◢ What am I reading about?
- ◢ Why am I reading?
- ◢ How am I reading?

☞ EXAMPLE: **Reading a novel**

What? A murder thriller.

Why? For pleasure.

How? From the first word to the last word.

☞ EXAMPLE: **Reading newspaper job advertisements**

What? Job vacancies.

Why? Looking for a job.

How? By locating the job advertisement section, looking through the section quickly to find suitable jobs, and reading those advertisements more carefully to find specific information such as qualifications needed and salary.

TASK 1

You have just bought a video cassette recorder and you want to know how it works. To do this, what do you read? How do you read?

Many students are only familiar with the 'from the first word to the last word' strategy. This is just one of a number of different reading strategies. The student of psychology quoted on the previous page was trying to understand every word in the passage he was reading. Since his purpose was only to understand the main points, his strategy was inappropriate and he was unable to complete the task.

In the Reading section you need to use a variety of different strategies to answer the questions. These are described in the section below.

OVERVIEWING A PASSAGE

Whatever your purpose for reading, you should always begin by getting a total picture or overview of the passage. The aim of overviewing is to see the 'forest' before you start to look at the 'trees'.

How to overview

- read the title and headings to understand what the passage is about
- look at the titles of any diagrams, tables, graphs and illustrations
- don't read word by word at this stage and don't follow the text with your finger or a pen
- don't worry about words you do not understand

Whether you are overviewing a book, an article or a two-page IELTS reading passage, you should never take more than two minutes.

After overviewing, you should know the topic: what is the passage about? You should also know the writer's purpose: is the writer, for example, describing a process, making a comparison, giving recommendations?

EXAMPLE: **The title of the passage you are going to read is '*Hope on the horizon for cancer patients*'. What do you think it is about?**

Simply from reading the title, it is possible to predict that the passage will:

- describe a new discovery (a drug? a surgical technique?)
- describe where/how/when/by whom/the discovery was made
- discuss implications for cancer patients: benefits/risks of the discovery

---

TASK 2*

From the following titles/headings, what can you predict about the passages which follow them?

1. Science Student Numbers Rising
2. The Overselling of Candidates on Television
3. Summary
4. What Economics Is
5. The Challenges of Studying Abroad
6. Study Abroad: a Manual for Overseas Students
7. Abstract
8. The Emergence of the Tiger Economies: the Pacific Century
9. Immigrants Positive for Economy
10. War of Technology Giants
11. Using Your Compact Disc Player
12. College Regulations

TASK 3

Choose a magazine or book. By overviewing the cover page(s), predict as much as you can about the contents. Check how accurate your predictions were by looking at the list of contents.

TASK 4

From the list of contents, select one article or chapter. Overview this in no more than two minutes. After you have finished, read all of the article or chapter to see how accurate your predictions were.

UNDERSTANDING THE MAIN POINTS

In each paragraph of a passage there is often a summary sentence which contains the main idea of the paragraph. The other sentences in the paragraph expand, illustrate, and/or explain this main idea. The summary sentence is frequently, though not always, the first or second sentence of the paragraph. If your purpose is to understand the main points of a passage you should locate and underline this sentence in each paragraph.

☞ EXAMPLE:

a) <u>It is difficult to make a distinction between food additives and food Ingredients</u>. Sugar, which is a natural product, is generally considered to be an ingredient whereas saccharin, an artificial sweetener, is usually termed an additive. One method of distinguishing between additives and ingredients is to classify them according to function. Additives are used in food production to enhance flavour and colour, to prolong shelf life and to preserve or enhance nutritional value. These functions are non-essential and hence it is possible to classify the substances which perform them as additives rather than ingredients.

b) Improved sanitation is not the only factor which accounted for the decline in morbidity and mortality rates. <u>In the period following the Second World War the use of the pesticide DDT had a profound effect on public health</u>. DDT was used to control the pests which spread diseases such as sleeping sickness, malaria and typhus. Used throughout the developing world, over one billion people were liberated from the threat of these diseases. Following the wide-scale employment of DDT in Sri Lanka in 1947, the number of deaths resulting from the disease fell from over 10,000 a year to zero in the early '60s. Ten years later, as a result of a reduction in the DDT spraying campaign, over two million people were infected with malaria.

c) It is probable that the characteristics of the annual growth layers or rings formed by trees reflect the physical conditions which existed at the time of their formation. As similar variations are found to occur in the annual growth layers of numerous trees in a given location it can be assumed that the common external factors which have caused these variations are related to climate. <u>As a result, the analysis of annual growth layers, a science known as dendro-climatology, provides a historical record of the climate</u>.

d) <u>After entering the body, the virus may lie dormant for up to six weeks. When it becomes activated, the body's immune system responds and the first symptoms may appear as a result</u>. These usually consist of a rise in temperature which may result in a fever and associated aching muscles and debilitation. Glands may become enlarged while the upper respiratory tract becomes inflamed. This constitutes the most dangerous phase for sufferers.

TASK 5*

In each paragraph, underline the sentence which gives the main idea.

1. Oceanographic surveys indicate that manganese nodules are present in large

continued on page 15

quantities on the seabeds of every ocean. Particles of manganese precipitate from sea water and adhere to sand or rock fragments, growing around the nucleus to form onion-shaped structures up to 10 centimetres in length. In shallow waters, nodules may grow up to one millimetre per year whereas in deeper waters the same growth may take a thousand years. The most conservative estimates suggest that half a million tons of manganese is located in nodule form on the floor of the Pacific Ocean.

2. The report reviewed three studies on the economic impact of immigration. It found that immigration generally provides some economic benefits to the nation in the form of an increased labour pool and consumer market. In conclusion, the report argued that, although the positive economic effects may not be significant, immigration did not have a detrimental effect on the economy.

3. Endemic goitre is commonly caused by an iodine-deficient diet. As a result of iodine deficiency, the functioning of the thyroid gland is impaired. The gland may then become enlarged and produce a swelling in the neck. A severely inhibited thyroid function may lead to a lower metabolic rate, stunted growth and the possible impairment of mental faculties. The disease is particularly common in mountainous regions of western China and northern India where the local soil and water are low in iodine.

4. When the study populations were classified according to World Health Organisation criteria for hypertension, a similar pattern to that described above emerged. Definite hypertension was more prevalent among urban populations for both ethnic groups and sexes than rural populations. Polynesian females had higher prevalence of definite and borderline hypertension than Caucasian females in the rural areas. Among urban males, hypertension prevalence was very similar for both ethnic groups, whereas among rural males prevalence of definite hypertension in Polynesians was only about half that in Caucasians.

TASK 6

Overview the passage below and be prepared to discuss the main points.

Word-Association Tests

The Background
Nineteenth-century associationist theories postulated that the mind functions in terms of association, forming sets of concepts and experiences. Associationists argued that mental contents could be studied by

continued on page 16

noting the links of similarity, contrast and proximity which exist in an individual's thought and behaviour patterns. Pavlov's notion of conditioning is itself based on the associationist theory that one stimulus becomes associated with another. If a bell is rung each time a dog is given food, the dog will become conditioned to salivate on hearing the bell ring, despite the absence of food.

Initially used to investigate the differences in cognitive styles, word-association tests became sensitive instruments for the detection of emotional concerns.

Methodology

In a word-association test, a subject is presented with a list of about 100 words as stimuli. Each word is read out by the tester and the subject is required to respond with the first word which comes into his or her mind on hearing the stimulus word. The tester notes the subject's response time for each of the words with the use of a chronometer.

Interpretation of Results

It is argued that if the subject is emotionally indifferent to a stimulus word, the response time for the reaction word is very short. If, on the other hand, the stimulus word is imbued with emotional significance for the subject, the response time is likely to be significantly longer. In addition, reactions to significant words may also include hesitation, stuttering, involuntary movement or other symptoms of disturbance. Jung, who used word-association tests in the early part of his career, showed that family members, in particular mothers and daughters and husbands and wives, exhibited similar responses to the same stimulus words. He argued that this indicated a failure to achieve individuation and was symptomatic of the potentially negative dynamics that exist in family relationships.

A Case Study

In a test carried out by Donald D. Jaffe, a pioneer of word-association tests, a subject was observed to exhibit delay and disturbance in response to the words 'friend', 'bottle', 'window', and 'fight'. Jaffe suggested that the subject had been involved in a drunken fight with a friend in which a window had been broken. The subject admitted that such an experience had, indeed, taken place and that the friend had sued the subject for damages resulting from injuries he had received.

UNDERSTANDING RELATIONSHIPS IN PASSAGES

Locating the summary sentence of a paragraph provides one way of increasing reading effectiveness. Other relationships also exist between words and phrases in a sentence, between the sentences in a paragraph and between whole paragraphs. Understanding and recognising these relationships helps you read even more effectively Some of the most common types of relationship linking ideas in passages are:

a) addition: adding new information

b) cause and effect

c) time

d) general and particular

e) contrast/comparison

In some cases the relationships are indicated by 'linking words'. In other cases, the relationships are not directly indicated and must be inferred. In the examples below, the linking words are printed in bold type.

☞ EXAMPLE:

a) Relationships of Addition: adding new information

Between words or groups of words

- Maize, millet, sorghum **and** cassava
- Solar **as well as** wind power
- Leukemia **in addition to** osteoporosis
- **Besides** nuclear fusion, nuclear fission **also** provides a source of energy

Between sentences

- The factor most commonly associated with driving accidents is excessive speed. The **second** most common factor is alcohol.
- Young children love playing computer games. They are **also** fond of watching TV.

Between paragraphs

- A tape recorder is a useful tool for the language learner. The learner can record herself making short speeches which can then be used (by either the learner or another person to pinpoint areas of difficulty in pronunciation and grammar.

  The learner can **also** record native speakers and use this data for language analysis. Some useful exercises are listed below.

- ... a total ban on whale hunting is, therefore, the only means by which the future of the species can be safeguarded.

  Another species which risks extinction is the Asian elephant. If hunting and poaching continue at the present rate ...

b) Relationships of Cause and Effect

Between words

- Any kind of constantly repeated movement of the limbs can **cause** the condition known as Repetitive Strain Injury or RSI.
- Overwork can **lead to** stress.
- Prolonged use of the drug can **result in** loss of memory and confusion.

Between sentences

- The credit rating of the South Tully Bank was downgraded by two points. As a **consequence**, many depositors withdrew their funds, which in turn led the bank to freeze all withdrawals for 60 days.

Between paragraphs

- The new pill XZ 23 can terminate pregnancy up to seven weeks after conception. The pill causes the uterus to contract, provoking a miscarriage. The advantage of chemical termination, researchers claim, is the avoidance of surgical intervention in which damage to the womb and post-operative trauma may occur.

  Critics, **however**, suggest that the pill itself may have equally damaging side-effects. They argue that XZ 23 can result in internal bleeding and may reduce a woman's future chances of conceiving. XZ 23 has been available for only the past seven years and Switzerland is the only country where it is commonly prescribed. Critics of the pill suggest that not enough research has been carried out to understand the long-term effects of its use and urge caution before adopting it in this country.

c) Relationships of Time

Between words

- Wash **then** cauterise the wound.
- Sediment removal occurs **after** grinding.

Between sentences

- Mortality data for the 1975–80 period were collected from various sources throughout the islands. Because some regions have inadequate death registration, the data were **then** adjusted for under-numeration.
- Subjects were asked to fast overnight and to present at the Survey Centre at 7.30 a.m. **On arrival**, a fasting blood sample was taken and a 75 g oral glucose load was administered.

Between paragraphs

- The first few minutes after a disaster occurs represent a critical phase in disaster management. In this phase the efficient collection and processing of information is essential to the implementation of an effective management policy. Information regarding the type of disaster, the immediate consequences and possible developments needs to be relayed to the Disaster Management Control Centre.

  Minutes later, on the basis of this information, the DMCC is able to co-ordinate all rescue and damage limitation operations. In this way it is possible to avoid ...

d) General and Particular Relationships

Between words

- Medieval cities **such as** Durham, York and Chester have fine examples of Norman or Gothic cathedrals.

  NOTE: In the following example, there are no linking words indicating the relationship.
- Kangaroos, wallabies and koalas are all members of the marsupial family.

Between sentences

NOTE: In the following example, there are no linking words indicating the relationship.

- After arriving in their new country, migrants are faced with many challenges. They may have to learn a new language, find accommodation and work and adjust to a different culture and lifestyle.
- The use of tranquillisers has reached unprecedented proportions in the United States. A recent survey found that 75 per cent of those interviewed had taken tranquillisers at some time in the previous year.
- The average woman's life expectancy is now eight years longer than that of the average man. Mary Crabbe, 73, has been a widow for five years since her husband died of a heart attack at the age of 69.

Between paragraphs

NOTE: In the following example, there are no linking words indicating the relationship.

- The Bedouin tribes of the Arabian peninsula evolved a lifestyle which was well adapted to the harsh desert conditions in which they lived. Their management of the desert's limited natural resources – wells, camels and grazing land – provided a difficult but sustainable lifestyle that was relatively unchanged from the time of Muhammad to the early 20th century The arrival of a strong, central government, an oil-based economy and a modern transportation and communications structure radically altered this traditional lifestyle.

  The Rashid of the Hadhramaut experienced a complete transformation of their lifestyle in under a generation. The mainstays of their economy until the 1950s had been camel breeding and the organisation of camel trains north to the Hejaz (supplemented by periodic inter-tribal raiding). The roads which were built in this period and the arrival of trucks almost immediately destroyed the basis of this economy As a result, many of the nomads settled in the booming oil towns which had developed and found jobs in this new sector. The centuries-old culture of the desert had disappeared forever.

e) Relationships of Contrast/Comparison

Between words

- arches **but not** vaults
- beans, **as opposed to** peas

Between sentences

- Tea contains caffeine and can cause insomnia. Herbal tea, **in contrast**, does not and is therefore a recommended pre-bedtime drink.
- Statistics show that inhabitants of New York are eight times more likely to be murdered than those who live in Little Rock, Arkansas. **On the other hand**, you are ten times more likely to die of boredom if you live in Little Rock than if you live in the Big Apple.

Between paragraphs

- Urban planning is subject to local and regional, not national, legislation. In the north, with its flourishing economy and highly developed infrastructures, comprehensive planning laws control all urban development from the building of a new freeway to the erection of a garden hut. Regional and local governments strictly enforce these laws and this has resulted in relatively controlled development despite a booming industrial sector which has increased its share of the region's GDP from 38 per cent to 76 per cent in under 20 years.

The south presents **a very different picture**. Although many of the local and regional laws are identical to those of the north the different economic conditions in the south have led to problematic planning outcomes. In a relatively non-industrialised region (industry accounts for only 12 per cent of the region's GDP) which suffers from high unemployment and net population loss due to emigration, irresistible pressures have grown to industrialise. In many cases, this has resulted in the flouting of planning laws, often with the tacit consent of government. The problem is further complicated by difficulties in enforcing the law where a desire exists to do so. Homes are frequently built without applications for planning permission. Were the government to enforce the law, this would result in the demolition of tens of thousands of illegally constructed dwellings, creating a political and social crisis that no government has yet been able to face.

TASK 7*

Study the following passages (A-H). What is the relationship between the sentences in each passage? Which words (if any) indicate the relationship?

A. Coal is transported from the mine to the power station by rail. After arrival it is stored in bunkers and then, when required, fed into large furnaces where it is burnt.

B. During the 1950s the expanding industries of the north required large numbers of unskilled workers. As a result, many migrant workers arrived from the economically depressed southern provinces in search of work and improved living standards.

C. Draining of swamp land is an important factor in the fight against malaria. The drainage of the Pontine marshes in the 1930s virtually eliminated the incidence of the disease.

D. Coal-fired power stations are relatively safe but emit large amounts of carbon dioxide and other polluting agents into the atmosphere. Nuclear-generated power, on the other hand, is clean but can, if things go wrong, lead to disastrous consequences.

E. The government's decision to close the unprofitable Liverpool car plant had two effects on the economy of the city. Firstly, 3000 people were made redundant, creating personal hardship and a severe strain on the social services. Secondly, many of the skilled workers left the area in search of work elsewhere, creating a serious shortage of skilled manpower.

continued on page 21

F. In the 1940s farmers were encouraged to use DDT and artificial fertilisers to eliminate pests, enhance soil fertility and hence increase crop yields. In the 1960s it became apparent that the use of chemicals in agriculture was causing serious damage to soils, plant and human life and this led to the banning of DDT in many countries and the search for more environmentally friendly fertilisers.

G. One of the most serious side-effects of the introduction of irrigation to formerly arid areas is the spread of disease. Schistosomiasis, an emphysema-like disease carried by parasitic larvae in aquatic snails, is now common in newly irrigated areas throughout the developing world and is believed to affect more than 200 million people.

H. The majority of landslides in the coastal areas of California are attributed to the instability of the Tertiary and Mesozoic rocks which predominate in this area. In inland desert regions, on the other hand, the major cause of slides is the extreme diurnal temperature range which results in cracking and the formation of talus at the base of rock faces.

Understanding the relationships between sentences in a paragraph and between paragraphs makes you a more effective reader and facilitates note-taking. You may find it helpful to make margin-notes as in the following example.

☞ EXAMPLE:

The Accumulation of Caesium 137 in the Food Chain

Chemical substances which are not involved in the process of respiration and are not excreted may become highly concentrated as they pass through each step of the food chain.

general — If radioactive materials with long half-lives enter the food chain, the high concentrations which accumulate in successive steps may lead to serious health risks. The radioactive isotope caesium 137, a product of nuclear fission, has a half-life of 30 years. Once it enters the body contained within food, it becomes distributed throughout the body's cells, accumulating two- or threefold during each step in the food chain. — *cause* / *effect*

particular — Evidence of this phenomenon was discovered by studies carried out in the Mackenzie Bay region of the Yukon in Canada where above-ground nuclear testing in the 1950s introduced large quantities of caesium 137 to the atmosphere. Rain caused the isotope to fall to earth, where it was collected by lichens growing in tundra areas. Tests on the lichen samples showed evidence of 6 micromicrocuries of caesium per gram of tissue. The lichens form the principal diet of caribou, whose meat is the staple diet of the Inuit peoples who inhabit the region. The caribou were found to have accumulated around 14 micromicrocuries of caesium per gram of tissue. — *cause*

Although only one step above the caribou in the food chain, the Inuit had concentrated up to 30 micromicrocuries per gram during the course of a single winter. Longitudinal follow-up studies have revealed a predicted rise in the number of tumours reported among the Inuit.

Glossary:

food chain: the cycle in which one organism becomes the food source for another organism, which is itself consumed by another

half-life: the time required for one half of a sample of unstable material to undergo chemical change

lichen: small plants which grow on the surface of rocks and trees

caribou: deer-like animals

TASK 8

Choose another passage and analyse it as in the example above.

TASK 9

Choose a passage and cover it with a card or sheet of paper. Move the cover so that you can only read the first sentence. What do you think the next sentence is? Use your knowledge of the relationships within passages to predict the content of the next sentence. Remove the card and see how accurate your prediction was. You can also use this technique to predict the next word or the next paragraph.

INTERPRETING DIAGRAMS, TABLES AND GRAPHS

Some reading passages may contain diagrams, tables and graphs. Because they do not give information line by line, they are sometimes referred to as 'non-linear texts'. Questions in the Reading section may require you to:

- match written information with a non-linear text (for an example, see TASK 11 on page 24).

- interpret the information contained in a non-linear text (for an example, see TASK 12 on page 25).

Many candidates become very concerned when faced with diagrams, tables and graphs.

IELTS: STRATEGIES FOR STUDY

You should remember that:

- Some non-linear texts serve only to illustrate the written text and no questions specifically relate to them. You can use the information they contain to help you understand the written text.

- If you are required to refer to a non-linear text, you should read it in the same way as you read any other text: overview it to understand the subject and check for the relationships between the points of information given.

- Remember that the information contained in a non-linear text can also be expressed in words. In order to perform the IELTS tasks which include non-linear texts, it is useful to mentally 'translate' the diagram, table or graph into words.

 EXAMPLE:

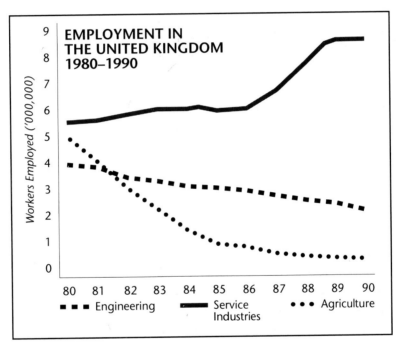

The graph can be 'translated' as follows:

The period 1980-90 saw significant changes in the relative sizes of three major employment sectors in the UK economy: engineering, service industries, and agriculture. There was a rapid decline in employment in agriculture, whereas employment opportunities in service industries increased sharply. The engineering sector, on the other hand, experienced a gradual but constant decline.

TASK 10

Select a diagram, table or graph and 'translate' it into words.

Which of the following passages, A, B or C, contains the main points in Table 1 below?

A. As a result of increasing urbanisation and consequent lifestyle changes, a shift took place in the mortality patterns of Dalwogen Islanders during the period 1960–80. While malaria was eradicated by the introduction of chemical pesticides, changes in the Islanders' diet and increases in the consumption of alcohol and tobacco brought about a sharp increase in the number of deaths resulting from tumours and coronary disease. Equally significant was the increase in the number of accident-related deaths.

B. Significant changes occurred in the mortality patterns of Dalwogen Islanders in the period 1960–80. Most striking was the increase in the number of deaths resulting from suicide, murder, and accidental causes. Similarly significant were the increases in the number of tumour-related and coronary-related deaths. Both of these trends can be explained by the rapid urbanisation of Dalwogen in the period in question.

C. The increase in the incidence of coronary disease among Dalwogen Islanders noted in Table 1 can be directly attributed to dietary and lifestyle changes. An epidemiological study carried out between 1958 and 1981 showed that the per capita consumption of sugar had increased by 800 per cent. In conjunction with the increasingly sedentary occupations in which the majority of Islanders were employed by the late 1970s, the incidence of coronary disease in the Islands had reached similar levels to those recorded in developed countries.

Table 1

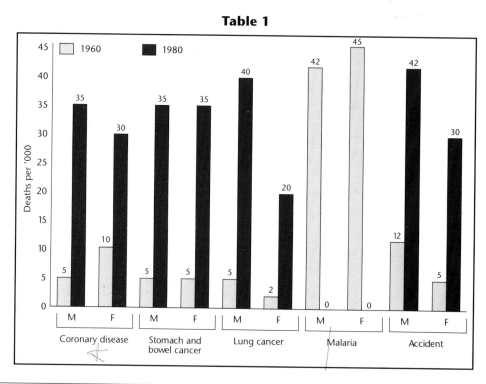

TASK 12*

Decide whether, according to Table 1, the following statements are true or false. Write T for true, F for false, or N if no information is given in the Table. Write your answers in the spaces provided.

1. The largest single cause of death in 1960 was coronary disease.

2. No malaria-related deaths among Dalwogen males were recorded in 1980.

3. Dalwogen Islanders had more accidents in 1980 compared with 1960.

4. In 1980 lung cancer caused the death of fewer Dalwogen males than did coronary disease.

5. The life expectancy of Dalwogen females increased between 1960 and 1980.

Write your answers here:

1. . . . .   4. . . . .
2. . . . .   5. . . . .
3. . . . .

UNDERSTANDING THE ORGANISATION OF A PASSAGE

Knowing how information is organised helps you read more efficiently.

 EXAMPLE:

If you are looking for a person's telephone number, the way that the telephone directory is organised—in alphabetical order—and your knowledge of the alphabetical system enable you to find what you are looking for rapidly and efficiently.

TASK 13*

The following is a list of the components of a textbook entitled 'Self-Instruction in Language Learning'. Arrange them in the order that they are most likely to appear.

bibliography	index
preface	table of contents
introduction	Unit 2
Unit 1	appendix
conclusion	

Within each of a textbook's components, similar patterns of organisation can be found. The purpose of an index, for example, influences the organisation of the information it contains. Its alphabetical order enables the reader to locate information rapidly.

Most people are familiar with indexing purposes and organisation. They may be less familiar with other ways of organising information which are common in academic writing. Some of these may appear in the IELTS test and you may be asked questions which assess your ability to recognise them. The following purposes are common in academic writing:

- describing processes
- examining advantages/disadvantages, benefits/risks
- describing/proposing solutions to problems.

There are conventional ways of organising information to achieve these purposes. Recognising these types of organisation helps you read more efficiently. The following passages describe solutions to problems. In both cases, the problem is described before the solution.

 EXAMPLE:

Extension of Riverflow Records in Thailand [extract]

Administrators, hydrologists and engineers require detailed records of past variations in riverflow in order to develop projects such as bridge construction, hydro-electric stations and flood-control systems. Until recently, however, most countries did not make accurately gauged riverflow records. Even where such records exist, they rarely extend for more than about 150 years, too short a period to provide enough data for an accurate determination of long-term trends and patterns of riverflow frequencies. Although rainfall data are usually more extensive, the gain in record length using precipitation data is generally only a few decades. Based on the records of tree ring growth, however, it is possible to reconstruct riverflow data over periods of several hundred years and, in cases where trees of this age still survive, up to 2000 years.

 EXAMPLE:

Mine Subsidence in Nottingham

Subsidence and its effects on surface-level structures poses serious problems for the development and maintenance of building stock in coal-mining areas. In the 1960s, rapid urban expansion in the city of Nottingham, situated at the centre of Britain's East Midlands Coalfield, led to the development of suburban housing over the sites of relatively shallow abandoned mines or deeper active mines. In some cases subsidence developed, resulting in structural damage ranging from minor cracking to the collapse of some dwellings.

Nottingham County Council engineers had two possible solutions to the problem. The safest but most expensive solution involved the filling of abandoned mine-sites with grout, a cement-based material consisting of a mixture of cement, ash and water which then provided internal support.

The second, cheaper method required the construction (inside the mine) of concrete piers which supported the rock strata. This procedure was unsuitable in cases where mines were located below the water table or where rock strata had been seriously weakened. The decision to adopt one solution rather than the other had to be taken on a case-by-case basis. In each case a decision was made by evaluating the degree of risk involved and the cost of implementation.

In 1969, plans were announced to build a regional hospital on a site approximately 12 metres above an abandoned mine working. Although surveys showed that the rock strata were intact and the mine working was above the water table, Council engineers opted for the safer, but more expensive, solution.

The base area of the hospital, 1000 square metres, was bored with a series of 250 drill holes, each 10 centimetres in diameter, which penetrated the mine cavity. The cavity was filled with grout above which a concrete pier eight metres in diameter was constructed. The drill holes were then filled with grout to form a solid column with a slab support.

TASK 14*

The passage below describes a number of problems associated with tree planting and the solutions to those problems. By referring to the passage, match the list of phrases with the problems and solutions. Note that more options are given than are needed to complete the task.

Problem 1 . . . .   Solution to problem 1 . . . .

Problem 2 . . . .   Solution to problem 2 . . . .

A. a tractor-driven planter
B. hand-planting is labour-intensive
C. one in five trees dies with conventional planting techniques
D. small rural agencies provided the funding
E. a cheap plastic tree guard
F. the UTC Industries tree guard costs 20 cents

New Technology in Tree Planting

The gradual deforestation of the riverine areas of south-eastern Australia has led to a number of damaging environmental effects. The immediate effect of the removal of root systems and overhead shelter is to expose the earth to wind attrition, resulting in soil erosion. Subsequently, when trees no longer remove groundwater, a second consequence of deforestation is a rise in the water table, resulting in a greater incidence of flooding and salinity. Both these problems pose a serious threat to agriculture, the most important sector of the region's economy. As a countermeasure, the Federal government launched an ambitious scheme to plant a billion trees by the year 2000. The project, however, encountered a number of initial difficulties.

continued on page 28

TASK 14*: *continued from page 27*

By using traditional manual planting techniques, the scheme would have required a massive number of workers (estimated at 50,000 over a 10-year period. This would have resulted in extremely high unit costs which were unrealistic for many of the small rural agencies who were providing half of the finance. In addition, the eucalyptus seedlings and young trees suffered a 20 per cent mortality rate as a result of disease, poor drainage and inadequate protection from wind, animals and birds.

Mechanical planters and tree guards provided two solutions which have significantly improved the efficiency of the planting program. UTC Industries of Birchgrove developed a tractor-driven planter capable of planting both seeds and saplings. The planter, nicknamed the Green Goddess, can drill, plant and water 5000 seeds or 1000 saplings per hour. It is operated by one person, requires little maintenance and costs around $20,000.

The mortality rate of young trees has been drastically cut by a tree guard also developed by UTC Industries. This simple device is composed of a sheet of PVC plastic costing only around 20 cents which is wrapped around the trunks of young trees. It provides support for the growing trunk and protection against sheep, cattle or other animals while special holes and channels in the plastic allow light and air to enter and concentrate water to the roots of the tree. In contrast to traditional stake and wire support and protection systems, the plastic guards are much cheaper and can be installed on site more rapidly. Experiments have shown that mortality in young trees can be reduced by almost 90 per cent using this system.

The purpose of the following passage is to present the case for and against woodchipping in British Columbia. The writer first presents the evidence which supports this practice and then lists the evidence against it. The final paragraph contains a conclusion in which her own view is expressed.

   EXAMPLE:

Woodchipping in Old-Growth Forests

In July 1990 the provincial government of British Columbia passed a law permitting woodchipping operations in the old-growth hardwood forests of the province's north-west. Designed to boost the local economy and provide a cheap source of paper, the woodchipping operations created a storm of controversy.

In a woodchip program most or all of the trees in a small, selected area or 'coupe' are felled in an operation known as clearcutting. Larger trees, suitable for the production of sawn timber, are taken to sawmills, while smaller trees and branches are taken to chip mills to be made into chips for pulping. The total utilisation of timber from a given area provides a number of advantages. It significantly lowers unit costs, introduces a new product, woodchips, to the local economy and utilises sawmill wastes, which were formerly burnt, as a further source of woodchips.

for:

1. total utilisation

2. clearcutting:
• regeneration (less destructive than fire)

3. access roads:
• better managemant
• firebreaks
• more tourism

4. finance:
• more fire detection
• more employment

The provincial forest services argued that clearcutting facilitates forest regeneration in the same way that wildfires do. In contrast to wildfires, which destroy everything in their path, clearcutting is also much less destructive of forest fauna. The development of access roads and the increased financial resources generated as a result of woodchipping also permit the forest services to provide better management of their forests. Access roads which must be built to clearcutting coupes also serve as firebreaks while increased funding enables the fire services to employ more personnel to detect forest fires. In addition, the industry provides employment for workers in the logging and processing industries and stimulates the growth of tourism by opening up previously inaccessible areas.

against:

1. flora/fauna damage

2. clearcutting:
• erosion
• salinity
• siltation

3. dependent on overseas demand (possibly unemployment, debt)

Opponents of the woodchipping operations argued that the flora and fauna of the forests would suffer irreparable damage as a result of the woodchipping itself and the construction of roads. They claimed that the clearcutting would lead to soil erosion, increased salinity, siltation and the eutrophication of adjacent waterways. Unique species including the black-fringed owl, now found only in the area, risked extinction with a consequent loss of genetic diversity.

The Conservation Society of British Columbia further argued that the exploitation of the limited remaining virgin reserves for short-term benefits also represented poor economic judgment. Returns on the large capital investment required to build the new roads, construct a woodchip mill and purchase the heavy machinery required for felling were largely geared to an overseas market, as 85 per cent of woodchip products were bound for export. Fluctuations in the rate of overseas demand could not, therefore, guarantee long-term returns on investment. If, as a result of prevailing economic conditions beyond the industry's control, these sales were lost, this would result in wide-scale unemployment and large debts for the contractor companies who had invested in plant and machinery.

4. negative visual impact (no tourists)

Finally, in response to the suggestion that a tourist boom would take place as a consequence of infrastructure developments, conservationists claimed that the visual impact of clearcutting was unlikely to attract holidaymakers to the region.

When the timber trucks moved in to start logging in the spring of 1991, they were met by groups of protesters opposed to the logging. Violent clashes developed between the loggers and protesters, necessitating the presence of large numbers of federal and provincial police. In an attempt to prevent further conflict, the provincial government placed a moratorium on logging until a commission of enquiry released its findings in the summer of 1991.

conclusion:
• economic gain not guaranteed
• certain damage

The situation in British Columbia presents a clear example of the tensions which develop when the economic interests of developers are diametrically opposed to those of conservationists. While short-term economic benefits provide a tempting solution to politicians faced with a slump in export earnings, there is no guarantee that the economic gains can provide a sustainable means of development. On the other hand, it is certain that a resource – virgin wilderness – whose value cannot be calculated in merely monetary terms will be irreparably damaged.

The passage below contains arguments for and against the use of wind power as a primary source of energy. Match the list of phrases A–H with these arguments and the conclusion. Note that more options are given than are needed to complete the task.

First argument 'for'......................   First argument 'against' ....

Second argument 'for'..................   Second argument 'against'..............

Conclusion ....

A. wind stations are ugly
B. need to increase efficiency and reliability of wind power
C. infinitely renewable, non-polluting source of energy
D. 10 per cent of Los Remos's energy requirements are provided by wind power
E. wind power is becoming an increasingly important source of energy
F. wind power is at present inefficient and unreliable
G. there are 150 wind towers in the Los Remos area
H. wind stations do not generate dangerous emissions

Harnessing the Winds

Wind-generated power, sometimes called aeolian power, offers many advantages for an energy-hungry society becoming increasingly aware of the negative environmental impact of conventional electricity-generating systems. In contrast to coal or oil-fired power stations in which the majority of California's electricity is produced, wind-powered stations have a minimal impact on the environment. They produce neither carbon dioxide emissions which add to the Greenhouse Effect nor do they contribute to the phenomenon of acid rain which kills the lakes and forests where it falls. Unlike nuclear plants, wind stations cannot become another Chernobyl or Three Mile Island.

Wind power, like solar, hydro-electric and tidal power, is an infinitely renewable, non-polluting source of energy and is becoming increasingly important in satisfying the state's energy needs. The swishing blades on the wind towers of the state's largest wind station near Los Remos already provide 10 per cent of the city's energy requirement.

The major drawback of wind power, however, is the unpredictability of the wind itself. No wind – no power. Even when the wind stations are sited on the windiest hills there is no guarantee that the wind will blow 24 hours a day.

Until ways can be found to store generated power that can be used when

continued on page 31

the winds die down, wind power will remain a supplementary source of the states energy. Present state-of-the-art wind towers still require a minimum windspeed of around 25 kilometres per hour to generate commercially viable electricity. It is expected that improvements in the technology will lower this speed and increase the efficiency of production. At present, however, high installation and running costs and low efficiency mean that wind power is not economically competitive with conventional fossil or nuclear stations.

Environmentalists are also concerned about the visual impact wind stations have on the landscape. In order to generate commercially viable quantities of electricity it is necessary to install a large number of wind towers. In the Los Remos scheme there are 150 steel wind towers, each around 30 metres high, covering a total area of 80 hectares. They are silent and safe but ugly, making the majestic Los Remos Range begin to look like Manhattan in miniature.

Harnessing the wind does offer a clean, renewable source of energy, but until technology increases the efficiency and reliability of the system it will not be able to replace conventional fossil fuel or nuclear-powered stations. The most likely forecasts suggest the development of systems which integrate the use of both wind, solar, hydro-electric and conventional energy sources in such a way as to maximise the advantages of each source. In the meantime, research must continue to improve the generating efficiency, storage capacity and reliability of environmentally friendly energy sources such as wind power.

The purpose of the following passage is to describe a process. The writer describes each of the stages involved in the process in the order in which they occur.

   EXAMPLE:

Poultry Processing

From the moment a chick hatches from its shell to the time it becomes a packaged chicken in the home freezer, each stage of modern poultry production is part of an integrated, automated system.

stage 1:
• chicks to broiler units

A parent flock of chickens provides a hatchery with a continuous supply of eggs. One week after the hatching, the young chicks are transferred to cages in broiler units. Four chicks are kept in each cage and a broiler unit may contain up to 5000 cages. The birds are fed on grain which is mechanically distributed to their cages. In six to eight weeks, the chickens reach the required processing

stage 2:
• conveyor
• stunned
• cutter

weight. At this stage, they are removed from their cages and attached by their feet to conveyor lines where they are electrically stunned before passing

stage 3:
• *blood/drain*
• *baths*
•*flailing*

stage 4:
• *evisceration*

stage 5:
• *cooling*

stage 6:
• *packaging*
• *storage*
• *distribution*

through a cutter which severs their jugular veins.

After hanging for a few minutes to allow blood to drain away, the carcasses are passed through scalding baths heated to 50°C for approximately 30 seconds. This begins the process of feather removal. Emerging from the baths, the birds are then mechanically flailed to remove any remaining feathers. The carcasses are then conveyed to the evisceration area. Evisceration was formerly performed manually but is now carried out by pneumatically driven evisceration lines.

In the final stage the carcasses are cooled by being passed through iced water. The birds are then packed and stored in refrigerated deposits and are ready for distribution to retailers. Up to 1000 birds an hour can be processed in this way, resulting in a dramatic increase in production efficiency and consequently lower prices for the consumer.

Glossary:

evisceration: the removal of intestines

TASK 16*

The passage below describes the stages involved in the separation of gas and oil. By referring to the passage, match the list of phrases A–F with stages 1–4.

Stage 1 . . . .   Stage 3 . . . .

Stage 2 . . . .   Stage 4 . . . .

A. injection of fresh water

B. removal of water and gas

C. reduction of pressure in separator vessel

D. an outlet channel is placed at the bottom of the vessel

E. separation of oil, gas and water

F. separation takes place near the wellhead

The Separation of Gas and Oil during Drilling Operations

After oil-bearing strata have been penetrated by drill holes, oil comes to the surface by means of natural drive, for example under pressure of dissolved gas. If gas and water are present, the separation of these substances must occur before refining can take place. The separation procedure is carried out in a pressurised separator vessel, generally located near the wellhead.

The separation process involves a gradual reduction of pressure in the separator vessel from the elevated pressure at which the oil/gas mixture emerges

continued on page 33

TASK 16*: *continued from page 32*

from the inlet pipe to normal atmospheric pressure.

During this stage the water, oil and gas mixture forms three layers. The heavier water sinks to the bottom, leaving the oil above it, while the gas rises to the surface of the oil. The gas is then removed from the vessel through an outlet channel located at the top of the separator vessel. It is then either released into the atmosphere or, if present in sufficient quantities, may be recovered for commercial use. Water is removed in the same way by an outlet channel placed at the bottom of the vessel.

After the removal of the water, it is necessary to test for the presence of remaining salt. In order to remove the salt, fresh water is injected into the tank which dissolves the salt and allows the entire solution to be removed, thus eliminating problems during the refining process.

TASK 17*

The paragraphs below are not in their original sequence. Using your knowledge of the relationships between paragraphs, place them in the order that you think they should occur.

A. In response to the shopkeepers' concerns, the Siena Chamber of Commerce organised a protest demonstration. The local newspaper (part-owned by a large department store in the centre of the city) carried editorials denouncing the decision while a petition was drawn up seeking a reversal of the council's decision. Candidates standing for the elections to the city council which were to be held in December 1985 campaigned on a single issue: to revoke or maintain Regulation 375.

B. Not everyone was so happy, however. Shopkeepers were convinced that their trade would suffer. Fewer people would come into the centre, they believed, if they had to rely on public transport. They argued that deliveries would be more difficult and that the city would lose its character and become a museum without a heart.

C. The new by-law was greeted enthusiastically by a number of interest groups. Environmentalists, worried about the polluting effects of cars; lovers of the city's medieval and Renaissance architecture, appalled by the constant damage done to the priceless monuments of the centre; and ordinary people, tired of the noise and danger caused by cars and motor- bikes dashing through the narrow lanes, all rejoiced.

continued on page 34

TASK 17*: *continued from page 33*

D. A survey carried out in 1987 showed that traders' earnings in the historic centre of Siena had increased by 15 per cent in real terms since the new law had come into force. The local paper, which had been so hostile to Regulation 375, now proudly boasts that the centre of Siena has the safest, cleanest and quietest streets in Italy Why, they asked in a recent editorial, don't the backward citizens of Rome and Florence pass the same enlightened laws?

E. The elections were won by the Social Democrats, a party which had run its election campaign largely on the issue of the maintenance of the new by-law. The law stayed in force and the reign of the motor car and motor-bike was not to return to the city centre.

F. In January 1985, when the Siena city council passed Regulation 375, a by-law which banned the use of private motor vehicles from the historic centre of this beautiful Tuscan city, public opinion was extremely divided.

CHECKING REFERENCES

In order to read efficiently you need to be able to understand the way in which words can refer to other words in a passage.

   EXAMPLE:

Irrigation schemes and livestock management projects frequently co-occur and both have been promoted as the solution to the problems of local economies. Their co-occurrence is logical, as in the case of the wet rice zone of Asia, where the relationship between these types of projects is well established. In semi-arid regions, however, their co-existence presents planners with new challenges.

In the preceding passage, all of the underlined words refer to 'irrigation schemes and livestock management projects'. Understanding such references is essential for the comprehension of passages.

TASK 18*

In the passage below a number of words have been underlined. Draw an arrow to the word or words they refer to. The first one has been done for you as an example.

Taking notes in university lectures requires specific skills. These include identifying main points, understanding tasks and deciding relevance and relationships. If the notes are to be useful they should be clear and concise. When you read them again several months later you have to be able to make sense of them. Some students try to write down everything in a lecture. This is not a useful technique: it shows that they have failed to understand the purposes of a lecture.

TASK 19

Choose another passage. Underline words which refer to other words or phrases and then draw arrows to the words and phrases to which they refer.

FINDING THE INFORMATION YOU NEED

In a wide range of study tasks and IELTS tasks you need to locate and extract specific information. When this is your objective, you should use the following strategies, which will help you to locate information efficiently and rapidly.

- focus on your objective, ignoring irrelevant information
- look in likely places. Knowing the organisation of the text will help to decide which parts of the text are more likely
- run your eyes rapidly over the text, looking for words and phrases associated with the target information
- use print style to help you. Names, numbers, italics, bold print, and upper-case letters stand out from the rest of the passage

Remember that the information you need to locate may be expressed in different forms.

 EXAMPLE:

If you are answering the question 'How is iron ore extracted from the ground?', you should search the passage not only for 'extracted from the ground', but also for synonyms such as 'removed', 'dig', 'extraction', 'removal', 'mining'.

TASK 20*

In the passage below, underline the information which answers the following questions:

1. What is the maximum number of students who can enrol in BUSL 210 in 1990?
2. Are there any 100-level units in Business Law?
3. Which sentence summarises the two major aims of units offered by the Business Law discipline?
4. Specialisation in which courses leads to recognition by the professional accounting bodies?
5. Give the full titles (course code and course title) of five subjects on offer in 1990.

continued on page 36

6. How many students take units in Business Law as a step towards becoming professional lawyers?

7. How many credit points are given for the Basic Business Law course?

Business Law

Units offered by the Business Law discipline have two major aims:

Studies in Law

The discipline offers a major sequence in law for candidates not seeking to become lawyers. The curriculum is designed to develop an awareness of the nature and role of law in society through a basic understanding of: legal institutions; fundamental legal concepts; philosophical, social, political and economic issues raised by a system of law; the process of change in law and the overall relevance of law to decisions made in both the public and private sectors. Legal obligations arise in every facet of human life, whether on a purely individual basis, or as a consequence of association with other members of society in industrial, commercial or interpersonal relationships. The units in law provide the foundation for becoming a more informed and effective member of society, and for a variety of careers in industry, commerce, government and education. This major sequence of units is particularly useful for students to combine with specialised study in another field within the school, such as economics or, outside the school, in an area such as education, politics, history, sociology, philosophy or even those physical sciences which are becoming more business management oriented. There are no 100-level units in Business Law, so attainment of a double major with Business Law is relatively easy.

In 1990 admission to BUSL 210, and hence to the full sequence of Business Law units, will be restricted to a quota of 80 students selected on the basis of previous academic performance. These students must satisfy the prerequisite of having gained 18 credit points and be concurrently enrolled in BUSL 212 and BUSL 213.

Business Law

The great majority of students taking units in the Business Law discipline do so as part of their education towards a professional career. A specialisation in BUSL 300, BUSL 301 and BUSL 320 leads to recognition by the professional accounting bodies when taken as part of the professional accounting sequence. These qualifying units cover basic legal concepts and techniques; commercial, business and company law; and revenue law. Students who wish to take this sequence commence their study with BUSL 350.

Subjects on offer by the discipline in 1990 will include:

continued on page 37

TASK 20*: *continued from page 36*

200 level

BUSL 210 Foundation in Legal Studies	3 credit points
BUSL 213 The Legal System	3 credit points
BUSL 212 The Civil Justice System	3 credit points
BUSL 250 Basic Business Law	3 credit points

300 Level

BUSL 300 Law of Business	3 credit points
BUSL 301 Law of Associations	3 credit points
BUSL 302 The Criminal Justice System	3 credit points
BUSL 320 Revenue Law	3 credit points

All of these subjects can be taken as part of the Studies-in-Law sequence.

TASK 21*

In the passage below, underline the information which answers the following questions:

1. The passage indicates four problems associated with relative scarcity. What are they?

2. Indicate five employment sectors for which an Economics degree may be relevant.

3. What other subjects may be studied in conjunction with Economics?

4. Is it necessary to enrol in ECON201 in order to enrol in ECON351?

5. What restrictions are placed on entry to 100-level Economics units?

Economics

Economics is a social science which studies how societies deal with problems resulting from relative scarcity, i.e. problems of allocation, distribution, stability and growth. It involves the analysis of production, distribution and use of goods and services in all types of societies. It is concerned with how economic systems are organised and with how decisions are made by individuals, business firms and governments. Because of the broad scope of the subject matter embraced by modern economics, a university education in this area may lead to a wide variety of careers in industry, commerce, banking, education and government service.

A student who completes a substantial and coherent study of Economics chooses from a wide variety of programs within the discipline, the choice depending to a large extent on the student's interests and goals. Some students may choose to

continued on page 38

TASK 20*: *continued from page 37*

follow a highly specialised program concentrating on a particular area, such as Econometrics, whereas others may prefer to acquire a broadly based Economics background. In some cases students may wish to combine a major in Economics with specialised study in another field within the school, such as accounting, finance or statistics, or in some other area such as politics, geography, law or sociology.

Although ECON303, ECON333, ECON339, ECON342, ECON349, ECON350, ECON351, ECON352, ECON353, ECON355, ECON356, ECON358, ECON360 and ECON365 are designated as 300-level units, students need not have completed ECON201 Macro-economic Analysis before enrolling in these units. Consequently, students may be able to include these at an earlier stage in their programs if they so desire.

Entry into 100-level Economics

For students entering Macquarie University in 1990 or subsequent years, entry into the 100-level Economics core units ECON110 and ECON111 will be subject to quota restrictions. Entry to these units will be guaranteed only to students who have entered Macquarie under the Bachelor of Arts (Economics) quota or under the Bachelor of Economics quota or to students whose entry qualifications were above those required for entry under these quotas.

All students permitted to enrol in ECON110 or ECON111 will, subject to prerequisite and co-requisite requirements, be allowed entry to any subsequent ECON unit. Students whose course of study has satisfied all requirements for the award of the BEc degree may, if they wish, graduate as Bachelors of Economics.

EVALUATING INFORMATION

In tertiary study, tasks may require you to do more than simply understand the main points and find specific information. You will also be expected to critically evaluate the information you read by distinguishing between facts and opinions. In the IELTS test, your ability to do this may be tested by asking you to determine a writer's point of view or to compare two or more statements and decide whether they have the same meaning.

 EXAMPLE:

By referring to the passage below, decide which of the following statements is correct .

A. The writer encourages students to bring their children to New Zealand.

B. The writer discourages students from bringing their children to New Zealand.

C. The writer neither encourages nor discourages students from bringing their children to New Zealand.

Advice for Overseas Students

If you are planning to bring your children with you while you are studying in New Zealand you should consider the following points.

It is essential to make appropriate visa arrangements for your child(ren) before leaving for New Zealand. Children arriving on tourist visas cannot remain in the country for more than three months.

Full-time study is extremely demanding, requiring a commitment of perhaps 50 or more hours per week. Naturally, you will need to consider the impact of this on your children. The university provides free child-care on weekdays but the number of places available is very limited. Extra facilities are available off campus on a fee-paying basis and you should expect to pay around $30 a day. If you wish to apply for university child-care you must contact the Student Centre at least two months before your arrival date.

Deciding whether to bring your children or not can be difficult. Although it can create considerable financial and practical problems, you should consider the stresses caused by separation.

In order to answer this question you need to find evidence for each statement.

Statement A:

The word 'encourage' does not appear in the text. This suggests that there is no evidence to support the statement. However, you should also make sure that the same idea is not expressed in other ways. In this case, other words and phrases which give the idea of 'encourage' include 'recommend', 'you should', 'you need to', 'it's a good idea to'. None of these examples occurs in relation to the idea of 'bringing children with you'. Therefore, there is no evidence in the text to support A.

Statement B:

The word 'discourage' does not appear in the text. There are also no words or phrases which express the same idea. Therefore, there is no evidence in the text to support B.

The correct answer is therefore C.

  EXAMPLE:

The following two passages provide similar information about killing seals, but have very different points of view.

Passage A: 'Every year thousands of baby seals are brutally and needlessly slaughtered to satisfy the demands of fashion.'

Passage B: 'The annual harvest of immature seals supplies the fur industry with a highly valuable raw material.'

The different points of view are reflected in the language chosen by each writer. This is illustrated in the following table, which compares words and phrases from the two passages as evidence of the writers' points of view.

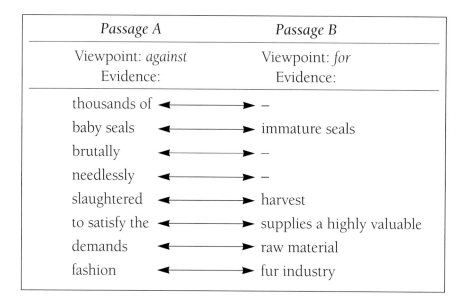

	Passage A	Passage B
	Viewpoint: *against*	Viewpoint: *for*
	Evidence:	Evidence:
	thousands of ←——→	–
	baby seals ←——→	immature seals
	brutally ←——→	–
	needlessly ←——→	–
	slaughtered ←——→	harvest
	to satisfy the ←——→	supplies a highly valuable
	demands ←——→	raw material
	fashion ←——→	fur industry

How does the choice of language by the writers of Passages A and B reflect their respective points of view?

TASK 22*

By referring to the reading passage 'Advice For Overseas Students' on page 39, answer the following question.

The writer believes that deciding to bring children with you:

A is an easy decision

B has a negative effect on your study

C needs careful thought

D has a negative impact on your children

TASK 23

Read the passage 'Woodchipping in Old-Growth Forests' on page 28 and 'Poultry Processing' on page 31. Decide whether the writers of these passages are in favour of, opposed to, or neutral about, the processes they describe. Provide evidence to justify your decision.

MATCHING INFORMATION

IELTS tasks may also require you to compare two sets of information and decide whether they have the same meaning.

EXAMPLE:

After reading a passage which contains the following information: 'The film's protagonists live in Paris, a small town in Texas.', you are asked to decide whether, according to the passage, the following statements are true or false, or whether no relevant information is given.

1. Paris is the capital of France.

2. Paris is a small Texan town.

3. Paris, Texas, is a beautiful town.

Remember that you are not asked whether the information is true or false in absolute terms or whether you agree or disagree. In this example, Statement 1 is false; Statement 2 is true, and there is no relevant information given regarding Statement 3.

 EXAMPLE:

Decide whether, according to the passage 'Advice for Overseas Students' on page 39, the following statement is true, false or unsupported by evidence in the passage:

'Bringing children with you causes considerable financial and practical difficulties.'

In order to answer this question you need to:

Find information which corresponds to the statement:

- bringing children with you causes considerable financial and practical difficulties. = 'It can create considerable financial and practical problems.' (paragraph 4)

Check how closely each part of each statement corresponds:

- bringing children with you = 'it'
- considerable financial and practical difficulties = 'considerable financial and practical problems'
- causes ≠ 'can create'

(Note: ≠ means 'is not equal to'.)

The verbs 'cause' and 'create' are synonymous. However, 'creates' means that bringing children with you always leads to problems, whereas 'can create' means bringing children with you may lead to problems, but is not certain to. This makes the two statements different in meaning and therefore the correct answer is 'False'.

When comparing two sets of information, check whether:
- the tenses of the statements correspond
- the verbs are qualified by an auxiliary such as 'can', 'must', 'should', 'might', etc.
- the facts are qualified by circumstances such as time, location, and manner
- the nouns refer to exactly the same things
- the same meaning is expressed with different words

Do passages 1 and 2 below contain the same information? What, if any, are the differences?

Passage 1

Most students in the Faculty of Science are required to write a 15,000-word thesis within two years of the commencement of their study. The thesis should contribute to the body of scientific knowledge and demonstrate an ability to undertake scientific research. In 1990 a total of six scholarships were made available to students enrolled in the Faculty of Science.

Passage 2

Science students may be required to write a 15,000-word dissertation by the end of their third year of study. The dissertation must contribute to the body of scientific knowledge and demonstrate the student's ability to undertake research. In 1990 a total of six scholarships will be made available to students enrolled in the Faculty of Science.

The two passages do not contain the same information. The differences are listed below.

tense:
'were made' ≠ 'will be made'

auxiliaries:
'are required' ≠ 'may be required'

circumstances:
'within two years of the commencement of their study' ≠ 'by the end of their third year of study'

reference:
'most students in science faculties' ≠ 'science students'

TASK 24*

Decide whether the passage 'Advice for Overseas Students' on page 39 supports, rejects, or provides no information about the following statement:

Full-time students may have to study for more than 50 hours a week.

TASK 25*

Decide whether the following passage 'The Role Of Pilot Error In Airline Crashes' supports, rejects, or provides no information about the following statements. If the statement is supported, tick box A. If the statement is

continued on page 43

rejected, tick box B. If the statement is neither supported nor rejected, tick box C.

1. The majority of major airline crashes in the period 1980-90 were attributable to pilot error. ☐ A ☐ B ☐ C

2. Five crashes in 1989 were caused by pilots ignoring ground-based electronic warning systems. ☐ A ☐ B ☐ C

3. All airlines will be required to install electronic warning units. ☐ A ☐ B ☐ C

4. The take-off phase of flight accounts for 4 per cent of flying time. ☐ A ☐ B ☐ C

5. Some pilots do not lower the plane's wheels before landing. ☐ A ☐ B ☐ C

6. Many pilots were unable to make rapid and accurate decisions during emergencies. ☐ A ☐ B ☐ C

7. Once the plane has reached its cruising altitude, the risk of a crash before completion of the flight is greater than the risk during the take-off and ascent phases. ☐ A ☐ B ☐ C

8. The approach and landing phases take longer than the ascent phase. ☐ A ☐ B ☐ C

The Role of Pilot Error in Airline Crashes

Research carried out by McDonnell Douglas, the US aircraft manufacturer, has found that almost 75 per cent of the 850 major airline crashes in the period 1980-90 were caused by pilot error. In 1989 alone five crashes resulted from the flight crew ignoring on-board electronic systems which warn that a crash is imminent. The Boeing report recommended that those airlines which did not possess the $30,000 electronic warning units should install them immediately and adequately train pilots to use them.

Although the final approach and landing phases of flights accounts for only 4 per cent of flying time, 40 per cent of the crashes studied occurred during these phases. The report recommended that safety procedures and pilot training should be improved to eliminate common pilot errors which resulted in crashes.

continued on page 44

TASK 25*: *continued from page 43*

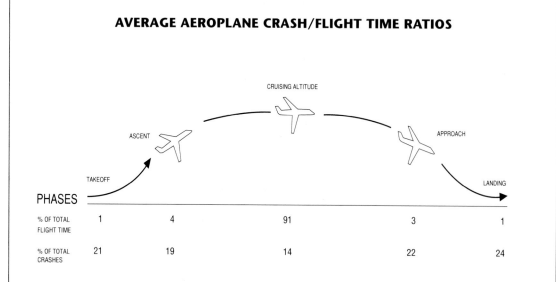

AVERAGE AEROPLANE CRASH/FLIGHT TIME RATIOS

PHASES	TAKEOFF / ASCENT		CRUISING ALTITUDE	APPROACH	LANDING
% OF TOTAL FLIGHT TIME	1	4	91	3	1
% OF TOTAL CRASHES	21	19	14	22	24

The report cited two examples of pilot error during landing. One of the most common causes of landing crashes is pilot failure to ensure that the plane's wheels are lowered before landing. In addition, it was reported that during emergencies some pilots found it difficult to make a rapid and accurate decision to abort or continue the landing.

UNDERSTANDING UNKNOWN WORDS

You may not understand all the words in the reading passages. Faced with an unknown word, some readers panic and believe that they will not be able to answer the questions Remember, however, that you often do not need to understand every word to carry out the required tasks

If it is essential to know the meaning of an unfamiliar word in order to complete the task, you should first check whether the word is defined in a glossary at the end of the passage.

It is also possible to guess the meaning from the context. One way of guessing is to use your knowledge of the possible relationships between words, phrases, sentences and paragraphs. The word you do not understand may relate to other words in the passage which you do understand.

☞   EXAMPLE:

Smoking is the major cause of _____ .

The unknown word is an effect of smoking. Your knowledge of the world tells you that the effects of smoking include lung cancer, bronchitis, emphysema and heart disease. The unknown word may be one of these.

TASK 26*

Guess the meaning of the unknown words. You may understand the meaning without knowing the exact English word. In this case describe the meaning with words you know.

1. The project team decided to _____ the conventional methods because they proved to be both too expensive and inaccurate.

2. Excessive consumption of alcohol can lead to disease of the _____ .

3. Holding your breath or drinking a glass of water are common cures for _____ .

4. The law permits private landlords to _____ tenants who fail to pay their rent for more than three months.

You can also look for definitions. The unknown word may be defined in the text:

☞ EXAMPLE:

In spite of intensive research, it is still not known why the _____ , the strange mammal with a beak like a duck, dies after short periods of captivity.

The unknown word is defined as a 'strange mammal with a beak like a duck'.

TASK 27*

Find the meaning of the unknown words.

1. _____ , or short-sightedness as it is more commonly known, ...

2. A _____ is a small tunnel used for accessing underground cavities.

3. _____ , also known as the Quetelet index, is defined as weight divided by height squared.

4. The _____ , or hereditary chief, acted as a legislator among the Treng tribespeople.

Opposite meanings may appear in the same text. If you know one meaning, you can sometimes guess the other. You need to look out for phrases like 'in contrast', 'on the other hand'.

☞ EXAMPLE:

_____ schools, as opposed to government-funded schools, are not required to submit annual staffing plans.

The unknown word probably refers to non-government-funded schools or private schools.

TASK 28*

Guess the meaning of the unknown word:

1. Northern Australia is subject to two kinds of natural disaster: in the wet season, the heavy rains cause flooding, whereas in the dry season farmers face the problems associated with _____ .

2. _____ , in contrast to the clergy, may bring a wider experience of life to a religious community.

3. Research carried out at Anchorage University suggests that _____ live longer than women who remain single.

4. Three national newspapers are published with a total daily circulation of five million. They freely debate all the major issues of the day. In contrast, before the change of government, the press was subject to strict _____ .

You can also use your knowledge and personal experience to suggest possible answers from the context.

☞ EXAMPLE:

In Western Europe the motor engine has now almost completely _____ the horse and the ox as a means of transport or source of power.

The unknown word probably refers to the idea of 'taken the place of'.

TASK 29*

Guess the meaning of the unknown words:

1. A recent survey of fatal car accidents in Venezuela showed that the main three causes in order of importance were _____, _____, and _____.

2. Any of the five permanent members of the UN Security Council has the power to _____ a decision made by the other four.

3. Over the past 20 years, digital watches and clocks have become as familiar as the more traditional _____ timepieces.

4. _____, commonly carried by dogs and foxes, was formerly fatal to humans who were bitten by these animals.

Deciding if the unknown word is an adjective, a noun, a verb or an adverb can help you guess its meaning.

☞ EXAMPLE:

The results of the research were extremely _____ .

The unknown word is probably an adjective. This limits the range of possible meanings: how can you describe the results of research? Other parts of the text will help to limit the range even further.

TASK 30*

Guess the meaning of the unknown words.

1. The results of the research were so _____ that the two researchers have been dismissed from their positions in the Institute.
2. The primary _____ of government subsidies are firms which specialise in hi-tech products.
3. Never _____ the wires if they are connected to the mains. Always make sure you are wearing rubber-soled shoes.
4. The car _____ on the wet road and crashed into an oncoming truck.

If it appears important to understand a particular word, do not rely on your vocabulary knowledge alone: always make a guess.

▶ FURTHER STUDY

The key to developing a further study program is to find appropriate passages and to carry out specific tasks on them.

FINDING APPROPRIATE PASSAGES

General Training Module

General Training Module passages reflect the many different kinds of texts you need to read when living in an English-speaking country. In order to find appropriate passages to practise reading, you should try to expand the list of examples given on page 8 and, if possible, obtain copies of these types of passages from newspapers, magazines and instruction manuals.

Academic Training Module

Books that introduce the reader to new topics, such as high-school and undergraduate textbooks, are useful sources of practice passages. In addition, English-language newspapers and magazines that cover technological developments and world issues can be used. These include *The Economist*, *The Guardian Weekly*, *The Far Eastern Economic Review*, and *Scientific American*. In preparation for tertiary study, you should also contact the institution where you plan to study and ask if pre-reading and course-reading lists are available.

DEVELOPING A STUDY PROGRAM

Exercises for independent study

Your study program should include regular practice of the reading tasks described in this unit. Each time you read, focus on at least two of the tasks from the list below. As you become more proficient, increase the number of tasks you carry out on one passage. Make sure your program includes the full range of tasks.

CHECKLIST

- overviewing a passage
- understanding the main points
- understanding relationships in passages
- interpreting diagrams, tables and graphs
- understanding the organisation of a passage
- checking references
- understanding the writer's viewpoint
- matching information
- understanding unknown words

Exercises with a study partner

Exercise 1

Choose a reading passage. Write a series of statements based on information in the passage, including some statements that do not contain the same information as the reading passage. (You will find it useful to refer to the Example below.) Ask your partner to read the passage and decide whether the statements you have written correspond to statements in the passage.

☞ EXAMPLE:

Since the mid-1970s, despite receiving external aid, the economy of Senegal has been in decline. Almost 50 per cent of export earnings are derived from the production of groundnuts, which account for half the cultivated land. As a result of the absence of adequate irrigation, the groundnut crop is highly vulnerable to seasonal changes in rainfall. The 1983 drought reduced production by over 70 per cent, with a devastating impact on the nation's economy.

Sample statements:	TRUE	FALSE
The Senegalese economy has improved due to external aid.	☐	☐
More than 50 per cent of Senegal's cultivated land is used for groundnut production.	☐	☐
The lack of adequate irrigation means that the groundnut crop is dependent on rainfall.	☐	☐
Crops in Senegal are vulnerable to variations in rainfall.	☐	☐

Exercise 2

Choose a reading passage. Write questions about the passage that require your study partner to locate specific information.

EXAMPLE:

Automatic teller machines (ATMs) are used by credit unions, banks, and building societies to facilitate banking transactions. They can be used to withdraw cash, to deposit cash and cheques, and to obtain an account balance. In order to access an ATM, clients require a PIN (Personal Identification Number). A recent US survey showed that around 50 per cent of ATM cardholders carry their PIN numbers with the card. This is in breach of the conditions of usage and makes the user liable for unauthorised use of the card.

Sample questions:

What does PIN stand for?

Which institutions use automatic teller machines?

Which practice violates ATM usage conditions?

According to the passage, is it possible to purchase goods through an ATM?

Exercise 3

Ask a study-partner to select a passage, make a photocopy and delete every sixth word. (You might decide to delete only every tenth word or, to make the task more difficult, every third word.) Your task is to guess the missing words. Check the original passage to see how accurate you were.

 EXAMPLE:

The passage selected by your study partner:

The report reviewed three studies on the economic effects of immigration and found that immigration generally provides economic benefits to the nation by increasing the size of the labour market and creating a larger pool of consumers. However, the size of these benefits is relatively small. In conclusion, the report argued that although the positive economic effects may not be significant, immigration did not have detrimental effects on the economy.

The passage you see:

The report reviewed three studies _on_ the economic effects of immigration _have_ found that immigration generally provides_____benefits to the nation by _____ the size of the labour _____ and creating a larger pool _o_ _x_ consumers. However, the size of _tou_ benefits is relatively small. In _____, the report argued that although ___t _he___ positive economic effects may not ___B_e__ significant, immigration did not have ___the___ effects on the economy.

Exercise 4

Ask a study partner to choose a short passage (no more than 50 words).

The study partner:

- numbers each of the words in the passage and retains this copy;
- makes a second copy, again numbering each of the words. This time the letters should be deleted and replaced with dashes. The study partner gives you this copy.

☞ EXAMPLE:

The passage selected by your study partner:

Word Processors

A word processor has three main components: a screen or visual display unit, a central processing unit, and a keyboard sometimes known as a data input unit. Word processors can be used to create, edit, store and retrieve information in a tenth of the time a manual system would require.

The copy retained by your study partner:

Word Processors

1 2   3   4   5   6   7   8 9   10   11   12
A word processor has three main components: a screen or visual display

13 14   15   16   17   18 19   20   21   22 23 24
unit, a central processing unit, and a keyboard sometimes known as a

25   26   27   28   29   30 31 32 33 34   35   36   37
data input unit. Word processors can be used to create, edit, store and

   38   39   40 41 42 43 44 45 46   47   48   49   50
retrieve information in a tenth of the time a manual system would require.

The copy your study partner gives to you:

Word Processors

1 2   3   4   5   6   7   8 9   10   11   12
— ——— ——— —— — ——— ————_: _ —— — ——— — ———

13   14   15   16   17   18 19   20   21   22 23 24
———, — ——— ———— ——, —— — ———— ———— ——— —— ——

25   26   27   28   29   30 31 32 33 34   35   36   37
——— ——— ——. ——— ———— —— — —— — ———, ———, —— ——

   38   39   40 41 42 43 44 45 46   47   48   49   50
———— ———— — — — — —— — ——— ——— —— ———.

Your task is to guess the missing words. For example, if you guess 'and', your partner will tell you each of the numbers where the word appears, in this case '18' and '37'. Fill them in on your copy and then take another guess, continuing until you have completed all the gaps. To make this task even more challenging, ask your partner to remove the title from the passage as well.

Exercise 5

You can also use Exercise 4 to increase your reading speed. Follow the same procedure as above but, before beginning to guess, ask your partner to show you the original passage for five seconds. The more you read (and remember!), the easier it will be to fill in all the missing words.

To help you understand more clearly which strategies you are using, you can also do these exercises in your first language.

TEST-TAKING STRATEGIES

Organise your time. The test paper gives you recommendations about the amount of time you should spend on each part of the Reading section. Even if you have not completed a task in the recommended time, go on to the next task. Many candidates achieve low scores in the Reading section because they do not follow this advice. Use the Sample Tests in this book to practise this skill.

Remember that questions may appear both before and after the reading passage to which they refer.

Read the questions carefully. Under the pressure of time and stress, some candidates begin tasks before they have properly understood what they need to do.

Try to answer all questions. There are no penalties for wrong answers.

MATERIALS FOR FURTHER STUDY

There are many textbooks available which are designed to help you to develop your reading strategies. You may find the following selection useful.

Abdulaziz, H.T. et al. 1989. *Academic Challenges in Reading.* Englewood Cliffs, NJ: Prentice Hall Regents.

Dobbs, C. 1989. *Reading for a Reason.* Englewood Cliffs, NJ: Prentice Hall Regents.

Garman, M. and A. Hughes. 1983. *English Cloze Exercises.* Oxford: Basil Blackwell. (This book practises gap-filling exercises.)

Haarman, L. 1988. *Reading Skills for the Social Sciences.* Oxford: Oxford University Press.

Nolan-Woods, E. et al. 1986. *Penguin Advanced Reading Skills.* Hammondsworth, Middlesex: Penguin.

Swan, M. 1976. *Understanding Ideas: Advanced Reading Skills.* Cambridge: Cambridge University Press.

Walter, C. 1982. *Authentic Reading.* Cambridge: Cambridge University Press.

MONOLINGUAL DICTIONARIES

Oxford Advanced Learner's Dictionary of Current English. Oxford: Oxford University Press. 1989 4th ed.

Longman Active Study Dictionary of English. Harlow: Longman. 1983.

Collins Cobuild English Language Dictionary. London: Collins. 1987.

Longman Dictionary of Contemporary English. Harlow: Longman. 1990.

Macquarie Concise Dictionary. Sydney, Macquarie Library. 1988.

IELTS: STRATEGIES FOR STUDY

▶ UNIT 2 *Writing*

This unit contains

'I had to write an essay about the advantages and disadvantages of nuclear-power generation. The question said "write an essay for a university teacher". I had two main problems – I wasn't sure what "generation" meant and I was also worried by the words "a university teacher". I've never even written a university essay in my own language.'

Chinese IELTS candidate

▶ WRITING TEST DESCRIPTION

In both the Academic Module and the General Training Module there are two tasks in the Writing section. The information in the following diagram applies to both the Academic Module and the General Training Module.

TASK	TIME	REQUIRED LENGTH
Writing Task 1:	20 minutes	150 words minimum (General Training Module)
Writing Task 2:	40 minutes	250 words minimum (General Training Module)

GENERAL TRAINING MODULE

In the General Training Module, writing tasks tend to be practical rather than academic. You may be required, for example, to write a letter of complaint, a letter seeking information, a statement of your study plans or a simple description of an aspect of life in your country. In writing task 2, however, you may also be asked to write about a contemporary social issue. Examples of General Training writing tasks are given on page 94 and in the *Practice Test Book* in Sample Test 4 on page 45. General Training Module candidates should pay particular attention to the following sections in this unit: 'Analysing the task' (page 58); 'Preparing a plan' (page 62); 'Collecting relevant information' (page 66); 'Writing up' (page 70); 'Checking your writing' (page 79); 'Diagnostic Tests' (page 88) and 'Test-Taking Strategies' (page 95).

ACADEMIC TRAINING MODULE

As in the Reading section, you do not require specialised technical knowledge to carry out the tasks. The writing test is designed to assess

- your ability to describe diagrams, tables and lists
- your ability to develop an argument supported by evidence
- your ability to communicate ideas clearly
- the range and accuracy of your English vocabulary and sentence structures

Writing task 1 requires you to write short descriptions based on graphs, tables or diagrams. Writing task 2 requires you to write about contemporary social issues of general interest.

SAMPLE WRITING TASKS

The following sample writing tasks are designed to familiarise you with the kinds of tasks you may be required to perform in the IELTS Writing section.

SAMPLE WRITING TASK 1

You should spend no more than 20 minutes on this task.

As society becomes more aware of the direct and indirect environmental costs of refuse disposal, the recycling of urban refuse has been perceived as an increasingly desirable and viable alternative. The diagram below shows how raw urban refuse can be recycled.

Task: As a course assignment you are asked to write a description of how urban refuse is sorted for recycling. Using the information in the diagram, write a description of this process and the equipment needed for carrying it out.

You should write at least 150 words.

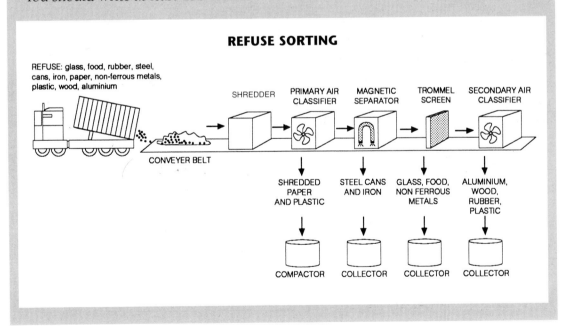

SAMPLE WRITING TASK 2

You should spend no more than 40 minutes on this task.

Children now watch more television than at any time in the past. Write an essay for a university lecturer considering its potential risks and benefits. Include recommendations.

You should write at least 250 words.

You should use your own ideas, knowledge and experience and support your arguments with examples and relevant evidence.

SAMPLE WRITING TASK 3

You should spend no more than 30 minutes on this task.

Increasingly large numbers of students are seeking to pursue their higher education in other countries. Clearly, the benefits are perceived to outweigh the inevitable difficulties involved.

Task: As a course assignment you are asked to write a brief paper discussing the advantages and disadvantages of studying abroad.

You should use your own ideas, knowledge and experience and support your arguments with examples and relevant evidence.

You should write at least 150 words.

▶ WRITING STRATEGIES

Each time you carry out an IELTS writing task you should follow a five-stage procedure:

Stage 1: Analysing the task
Stage 2: Preparing a plan
Stage 3: Collecting relevant information
Stage 4: Writing up
Stage 5: Checking your writing

STAGE 1: ANALYSING THE TASK

Do not start writing immediately. It is essential that you take at least a few minutes to make sure that you fully understand what is required by the task. To do this you must answer three questions:

- What is the question?
- Who is the audience?
- What are the task requirements?

TASK 3*

Underline the words which indicate the purpose of the following questions. The first two have been done for you as examples.

What are the stages involved in the refining of crude oil into petroleum?

Is a knowledge of essay writing necessary for students in tertiary education?

1. How do wage increases contribute to inflation?
2. How is crude oil refined into petrol?
3. What are the benefits and risks associated with tropical logging?
4. What are the factors which are related to anxiety in high-school students?
5. What kind of listening challenges do overseas students face in tertiary education? What recommendations would you offer?
6. Do the advantages derived from the use of chemical additives in food processing outweigh the disadvantages?

TASK 4*

In the following questions, circle the topic words and underline the words which indicate the purpose. The first two have been done for you as examples.

Do the benefits of study abroad justify the difficulties?

What advice would you offer to a prospective student?

1. Should the laws which prohibit the sale and consumption of heroin be applied to tobacco?
2. In your opinion should government intervene in the rights of the individual with regard to family planning?
3. What are the effects of the unrestricted use of private cars in urban areas? What recommendations would you make to improve the current situation?
4. To what extent has the diet of Melanesians changed over the past 20 years? What effects has this had on their patterns of mortality?
5. In what circumstances can capital punishment be justified?

Understanding 'to what extent' questions

Some questions, such as 'How is hygiene ensured in the production of cheese?' and 'What were the causes of the Great Depression?', can be answered with a series of facts. Other questions, such as 'To what extent has the diet of Melanesians changed over the past 20 years?' and 'How far does a knowledge of statistics contribute to success in tertiary study?' require an answer expressed in terms of degree: for example, 'The diet of Melanesians has changed to a great extent/very significantly/ minimally/not at all/etc.'.

Questions requiring an answer expressed in terms of degree can be asked in many different ways: in all of the following examples, both the topic and the purpose are very similar.

 EXAMPLES:

1. To what extent is a knowledge of statistics indispensable for study in tertiary institutions?

2. How far does a knowledge of statistics contribute to success in tertiary study?

3. To what degree is a knowledge of statistics useful in tertiary study?

4. 'A knowledge of statistics is indispensable for study in tertiary institutions.' Discuss.

5. What level of statistical knowledge is necessary for tertiary study?

These questions cannot be answered with 'yes' or 'no'. In order to answer them, it is useful to 'translate' them into questions which can be given a 'yes' or 'no' answer. This will help in the next stage of writing: preparing a plan.

 EXAMPLE:

To what degree is a knowledge of statistics useful in tertiary study? = Is a knowledge of statistics useful in tertiary study?

To what extent has the diet of Melanesians changed over the past 20 years? = Has the diet of Melanesians changed over the past 20 years?

To what extent is environmental damage irreversible? = Is environmental damage irreversible?

How necessary is media censorship in a modern society? = Is media censorship necessary in a modern society?

TASK 5*

Translate the following questions into 'yes/no' questions.

1. To what extent has the traditional male role changed in the past 20 years?
2. To what degree are coronary diseases preventable?
3. To what extent is diet a contributory factor in stomach and bowel tumours?
4. How acceptable are the risks involved in genetic engineering?
5. To what extent will migration from the developing world to the developed world become a social and political issue in the 21st century?
6. To what extent should the decision to suspend a life support system rest with a doctor?

There is no right or wrong answer to this type of question. During Stage 3 ('Collecting relevant information'), you will examine the evidence for 'yes' and the evidence for 'no' and draw an appropriate conclusion.

Translating instructions into questions

Some IELTS writing tasks may contain instruction words, rather than questions. Examples of instruction words include 'describe', 'discuss', 'evaluate', 'analyse', 'consider', 'make recommendations', 'explain', 'write a report'. This method of task presentation is particularly common in tertiary study.

 EXAMPLE:

Describe the stages by which crude oil is refined into petroleum.

Write a report for your sponsoring agency describing the English-language skills overseas students require. Make any recommendations you feel are necessary.

Analyse the effect of wage increases on inflation.

This method of presenting tasks is simply another way of asking a question. You need to 'translate' the instructions into questions.

 EXAMPLES:

Describe the stages by which crude oil is refined into petroleum. = What are the stages involved in the refining of crude oil into petroleum?

Essay-writing skills are essential in tertiary education. Discuss. = Is a knowledge of essay writing necessary for students in tertiary education?

Analyse the effect of wage increases on inflation. = How do wage increases contribute to inflation?

TASK 6*

Translate the following instructions into questions.

1. 'Nuclear deterrence has saved the world from war.' Discuss.
2. 'The dominance of black people in US sport is due to sociological rather than physiological factors.' Discuss.
3. Describe the ways in which relative costs have created terraced farming in Japan and extensive farming in Canada.
4. Explain why climatic conditions resist prediction.

Who is the *audience?*

The Writing section assesses your ability to carry out academic writing. The audience, therefore, will generally be a university teacher. You may also be required to write a brief report for an agency such as a sponsoring authority or a university administration. The writing tasks tell you the audience you are writing for. (See Sample Writing Tasks on pages 55 to 58.)

In the Academic Module, it is unlikely that your audience would be a friend, relative or private individual. As a result, your writing style should be appropriate to a formal audience. You should not refer directly to your audience as you would in a letter, e.g. 'Dear Sir'; 'To Whom it May Concern; 'To the X Sponsoring Agency', etc.

What are the task *requirements?*

You must

- answer the question set by following the task instructions exactly
- produce the required minimum number of words (150/250)
- use the information sources indicated in the task:
  diagrams or notes in the Writing section;
  your own knowledge and experience.

Do not go on to Stage 2 until you have thoroughly analysed the question.

STAGE 2: PREPARING A PLAN

When you have analysed the task (by understanding the topic and purpose of the question, the intended audience, and the task requirements, you are ready to prepare a plan. In a 20-minute task this should take about three minutes and in a 40-minute task about five or six minutes.

The analysis which you have made of the question's topic and purpose forms the framework of your plan.

How to write a plan:

1. Write the topic at the top of the plan. This will help to focus your planning.

2. Write the word 'introduction'.

3. Use your analysis of the purpose to provide the key ideas that will form the basis of your answer.

4. Write the word 'conclusion'.

  EXAMPLE:

What are the stages involved in the refining of crude oil into petroleum?

PLAN

Refining crude oil into petroleum

introduction:

stage 1:

continued on page 63

IELTS: STRATEGIES FOR STUDY

continued from page 62

> *stage 2:*
>
> *stage 3:*
>
> *stage ?:*
>
> *conclusion:*

In this example the key ideas are stages in a process. In other essay plans they might be problems, advantages and disadvantages, benefits and risks. Note that, before you have collected your information, you do not know how many stages, problems, advantages, etc. you will find. It is useful, therefore, to keep your plan open. As a general rule, you should expect to find at least two or three stages, problems, advantages, etc. To remind yourself that there may be more, use a question mark in your plan, as in the example above.

Note that all plans must include an introduction and a conclusion. The writing of introductions and conclusions is discussed in Stage 4.

 EXAMPLE:

What are the advantages and disadvantages of banning the use of private motor vehicles in city centres?

PLAN

> *Banning the use of private motor vehicles in city centres*
>
> *introduction:*
>
> *advantage 1:*
>
> *advantage 2:*
>
> *advantage 3:*
>
> *disadvantage 1:*
>
> *disadvantage 2:*
>
> *disadvantage 3:*
>
> *disadvantage ?:*
>
> *conclusion:*

☞ EXAMPLE:

To what extent is a knowledge of statistics essential for study in tertiary institutions?

PLAN

Knowledge of statistics in tertiary institutions

introduction:

essential?
yes: reason 1:
yes: reason 2:
yes: reason ?:

essential?
no: reason 1:
no: reason 2:
no: reason ?:

conclusion:

☞ EXAMPLE:

Write a report describing the benefits and risks associated with the use of air-conditioning in hospitals. Make any recommendations you feel are necessary.

PLAN

Use of air-conditioning in hospitals

introduction:

benefit 1:
benefit 2:
benefit ?:

risk 1:
risk 2:
risk ?:

conclusion = recommendation 1
             recommendation 2
             recommendation ?

This kind of plan is useful for comparing and contrasting points of view.

In Writing task 1, when you are required to describe the information contained in a diagram or table, you may find there is no question to analyse since the instructions may say something like "describe the following diagram". But you can – and should – still make a writing plan. In order to develop a plan you need to see how the topics are contained in the diagram, table or accompanying text.

☞ EXAMPLE:

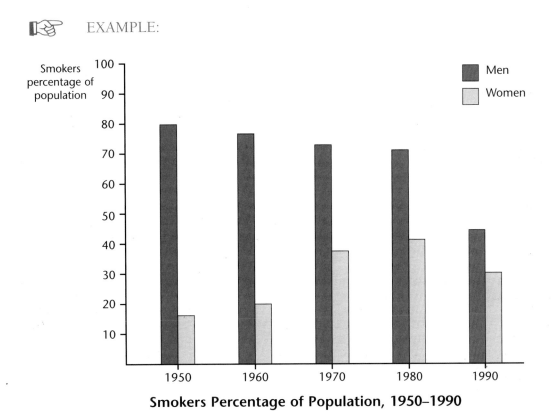

Smokers Percentage of Population, 1950–1990

TASK 7

Analyse the following questions and prepare plans.

1. To what extent is the use of animals in scientific research acceptable?

2. 'The dominance of black people in US sport is due to sociological rather than physiological factors.' Discuss.

3. Should the same laws which prohibit the sale and consumption of heroin be applied to tobacco?

4. Do the benefits of study in a foreign language justify the difficulties? What advice would you offer to a prospective student?

5. Write a report for your sponsoring agency describing the English-language skills overseas students require. Make any recommendations you feel are necessary.

continued on page 66

continued from page 62

6. In what ways has information technology changed work and working practices in the past 10 years?

7. To what extent should economic planning be influenced by the need for environmental conservation?

8. 'Foreign-language instruction should begin in kindergarten.'
Discuss.

STAGE 3: COLLECTING RELEVANT INFORMATION

Writing Task 1

In writing task 1 you should fill in the essay plan you developed in stage 2 by drawing on information contained in the diagrams, tables or lists which appear in the writing section. In this task the relevant information is provided for you and you must include all of it in your answer. To do this you need to be able to "read" the diagram, making sure you understand what its key points are. Most importantly, you need to be able to describe the overall trends described in the diagram. For example, in describing the following graph it is not sufficient to write "in 1960 there were about nine thousand marriages in Scotland, in 1970 there were about three thousand marriages, in 1980 there were three thousand five hundred marriages" and so on. Instead, you need to describe the changes that took place.

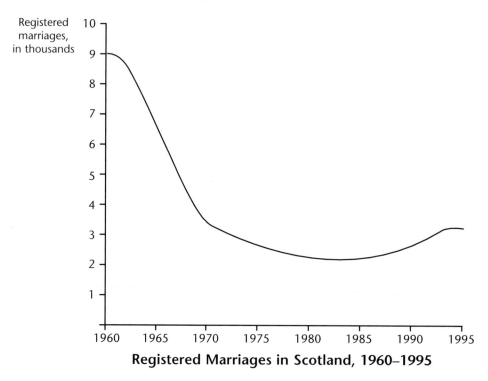

Registered Marriages in Scotland, 1960–1995

Sample Answer

The number of marriages in Scotland fell very sharply between 1960 and 1970, and continued to decline until around 1985 though at a slower rate. From 1985 onwards there was a gradual increase in the number of marriages which then levelled off in 1994.

TASK 8*

Describe the trends in the following graphs.

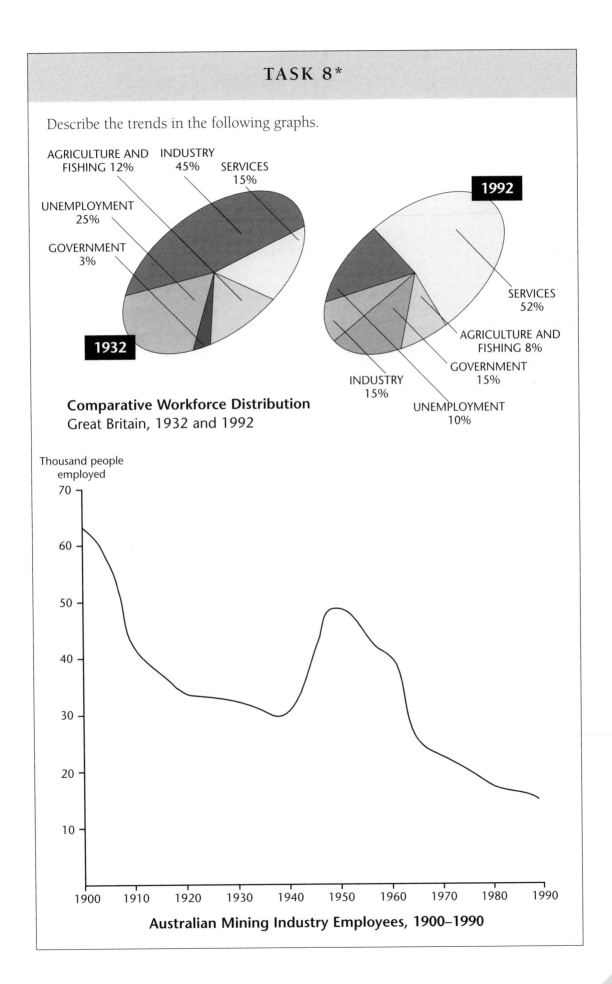

Comparative Workforce Distribution
Great Britain, 1932 and 1992

AGRICULTURE AND FISHING 12%
INDUSTRY 45%
SERVICES 15%
UNEMPLOYMENT 25%
GOVERNMENT 3%
1932

1992
SERVICES 52%
AGRICULTURE AND FISHING 8%
GOVERNMENT 15%
INDUSTRY 15%
UNEMPLOYMENT 10%

Thousand people employed

Australian Mining Industry Employees, 1900–1990

Writing Task 2

In writing task 2, you need to use your own knowledge and experience to supply the information for your writing plan. The following example shows how a writer used her plan as a guide to developing a plan for an essay about the English-language skills required by overseas students.

SAMPLE WRITING TASK

> You should spend no more than 40 minutes on this question.
>
> **Task: Write a report for your sponsoring agency describing the English-language skills overseas students require. Make any recommendations you feel are necessary.**

You should use your own ideas, knowledge and experience and support your arguments with examples and relevant evidence.

    EXAMPLE:

English-language skills overseas students require

introduction:

skill 1:   reading journal articles/books/ critically evaluating content

skill 2:   writing assignments (analysing the question, clarifying topic and purpose, taking notes from books, journals, writing up)

skill 3:   speaking in seminars/tutorials. Presenting ideas, asking questions, discussing with teachers and fellow students.

skill 4:   listening to lectures/taking notes

recommendations:

1. do language course before starting.

2. attend language classes during course.

3. find a study partner

conclusion

PLAN

Some students, particularly in exam conditions, find it difficult to think of appropriate examples. The questions contained in writing task 2 deal with contemporary problems and issues you've probably already heard about and have perhaps given some thought to. Remember, your ideas don't need to be original, only relevant to the answer. If it is difficult for you to think of examples you might find it helpful to focus on some specific aspects of the topic. For example, in answering the question about TV on page 58 you might start by thinking about the different kinds of program you're familiar with:

documentaries	feature films	news	weather drama
comedy shows	cartoons	educational TV	concerts advertisements

You can then consider the benefits and risks of each kind of program grouping all the benefits together and then all the risks.

☞ EXAMPLES:

documentaries
benefits: news- keeps people informed. Teaches children about the world
risks: may expose children to scenes of violence/ other frightening images.

feature films
benefits: a source of entertainment
risks: the films may contain themes and ideas which are unsuitable for children.

educational TV
benefits: teaches (and entertains) children – can improve reading, writing, develop imagination..

TASK 9*

Develop the following essay plan, adding as many reasons as you can.

Many people claim that the benefits of computers to modern society far outweigh the disadvantages. Do you agree? Write an essay for a university lecturer outlining the pros and cons of computer use.

advantage 1:

advantage 2:

advantage 3:

advantage ?:

disadvantage 1:

disadvantage 2:

disadvantage 3:

STAGE 4: WRITING UP

In tertiary writing, all essays should begin with an opening paragraph (an introduction), which may include a:

- setting (background information)
- statement of purpose
- definition of key terms
- summary of main points

 EXAMPLE:

setting — Since World War II popular American sports such as Baseball, Basketball and Field and Track have seen the qualitative and quantitative dominance *definition* — of black (Afro-American) athletes. The purpose of this essay is to examine — *purpose* the relative importance of the sociological and physiological factors which have contributed to this phenomenon. It will be argued that, despite some tentative evidence of physiological differences, the factors which determine — *summary of main points* black pre-eminence in sport are primarily sociological.

Introduction to an undergraduate sociology essay

In each of the following introductions the summary of the essay's main point has been underlined.

 EXAMPLE:

1. Should the laws which prohibit the sale and consumption of heroin be applied to tobacco?

Both heroin and tobacco are addictive drugs which can cause either death or serious damage to health. Ironically, although tobacco use is legal and heroin use generally illegal, far more people die as a result of smoking than as a result of heroin use.

At the same time, the tobacco industry provides jobs for many thousands of workers in the agricultural sector, the manufacturing industry and distribution and sales areas. If the same laws which are applied to heroin were applied to tobacco many thousands of workers would find themselves unemployed or forced to engage in illegal activities. <u>Providing a number of safeguards are put in place the present laws should be maintained</u>. Among these safeguards we must first consider.........

2. What are the benefits and risks associated with tropical logging?

<u>Tropical logging provides many short term benefits for the economies of developing countries and many long term risks for their environments and their economies</u>. Logging provides jobs and can earn valuable export dollars. It can also lead to deforestation, soil erosion and even climatic change. Until governments realise that their forests constitute a form of natural capital they will continue to exploit them unsustainably.

3. **Do the advantages derived from the use of chemicals in food production and processing outweigh the disadvantages?**

   <u>The answer to this question depends on whether it is being asked in the context of the developing or the developed world.</u> We all want good quality food at low prices. In order for food producers to meet this demand it has become necessary to use chemical fertilisers to increase production as well as additives to increase the shelf life of food and to enhance its attractiveness in terms of taste or colour. But the use of chemicals may also be very dangerous for consumers since they may build up in the body over a number of years. However, in those areas of the world where people are faced with starvation because of crop failure or inadequate levels of productivity the use of chemicals to increase production and to maintain the product in an edible state is very attractive. Risks associated with their use may as result be considered only secondarily. Consumers in developed countries can decide whether the benefits of low cost, readily available food outweigh the possible risks to health. In developing countries people often have no such choice.

TASK 10*

In the following essay extracts underline the sentence(s) which summarise the writer's point of view.

1. **The private car should be banned from all city centres.**
   In an ideal world we would have no cars in any of our city centres. Cars are dirty and noisy, creating smog which can seriously affect people's health. They are also dangerous; every year many thousands of people—both motorists and pedestrians—die in car accidents. Even though they cause death, illness and stress cars also seem to be indispensable to our lives. We use cars to go to work, to the cinema, to a restaurant. In cities without adequate public transport systems the car is essential for movement. If cars were to be banned from city centres many people would be unable to go to work, unable to go to places of entertainment; the economy of the city would be affected and the quality of people's lives would suffer.
   Providing various common sense rules are adopted cars should not be banned from city centres. These rules include.....

2. **Voluntary euthanasia should be legalised.**
   Voluntary euthanasia, the practice of allowing people to choose when and how to die, has recently become the subject of intense debate in many countries. Some argue that no-one should have the right to take their own life and that no-one should be able to help them either. Others argue that the right to die

continued on page 72

continued from page 71

with dignity and with as little pain as possible is a fundamental human right which should be respected and facilitated by the law.

In this essay I will argue that voluntary euthanasia represents a major threat to the individual and should certainly not be legalised. Once it becomes legal to assist another person to die it becomes difficult to know where to draw the line.

All IELTS writing tasks should also begin with an introduction. Because these writing tasks are relatively short, in most cases it is only necessary to write a one- or two- sentence summary of the main points contained in your plan. This is your introduction.

 EXAMPLE:

There appear to be both sociological and physiological factors which account for the dominance of black athletes in some American sports.

To copy from hard disk to diskette, the following procedure should be used.

There are four stages involved in the refining of crude oil into petroleum.

Although air-conditioning has clearly established benefits, it also introduces an element of risk.

TASK 11

Write introductions for the following questions.

1. Write a report to your sponsoring agency describing the accommodation problems faced by foreign students in Britain. Make any necessary recommendations.

2. How far does a knowledge of statistics contribute to success in tertiary study?

3. Write a report for your sponsoring agency describing the English-language skills overseas students require. Make any recommendations you feel are necessary.

4. Should the same laws which prohibit the sale and consumption of heroin be applied to tobacco?

Writing up the main points

Each of the main points in the plan should form the basis for a paragraph, as in the example following.

PLAN

English-language skills required by overseas students

introduction:

skill 1: reading journal articles/books/ critically evaluating content

skill 2: writing assignments (analysing the question, clarifying topic and purpose, taking notes from books, journals, writing up)

skill 3: speaking in seminars/tutorials. Presenting ideas, asking questions, discussing with teachers and fellow students.

skill 4: listening to lectures/taking notes

recommendations:

1. do language course before starting.

2. attend language classes during course.

3. find a study partner

conclusion:

Sample write-up of introduction and first main point:

Overseas students whose first language is not English face a number of language-related challenges in tertiary study. They need to have effective writing, reading, speaking and listening strategies.

All tertiary courses require students to write clearly and critically. This involves not only a command of the language system, but also an understanding of the conventions of academic writing.

Strategies for writing paragraphs:

1. Begin each paragraph with a summary sentence – a sentence which contains the main point of the paragraph.

2. Continue the paragraph by giving more information about the main point. This might involve: giving an explanation; an example; a reason; additional detail.

 EXAMPLE:

summary sentence → AII tertiary courses require students to write clearly and critically. This involves not only a command of the language system but also an understanding of the conventions of academic writing. ← *additional detail*

TASK 12

Read the following question and then, using the plan below, write a summary sentence for each of the main points contained in it.

Task: How far should society's economic needs form the basis of university curriculum?

PLAN

Society's Economic Needs/University Curriculum

Introduction:

should form the basis

yes, reason 1: train young people for employment

reason 2: help national economy through research

no, reason 1: society has important non-economic needs – medicine, law, etc

reason 2: education should teach how to think

reason 3: needs of employment constantly changing

conclusion: Education should serve society. Economic needs important, but not the only important need.

TASK 13*

By using the plan below, write the first three paragraphs of your answer to the following question.

Task: Write a report to your sponsoring agency describing the accommodation problems faced by foreign students in Britain. Make any necessary recommendations. You must write at least 250 words.

Accommodation for Foreign Students

introduction:

problem 1: limited on-campus accommodation, most students required to find houses and flats off-campus

problem 2: rents generally very high, difficult to find cheap and desirable accommodation

continued on page 75

continued from page 74

> *problem 3: property often unfurnished, difficult to find cheap furniture*
>
> *recommendations:*
>
>   *1. apply early for on-campus accommodation*
>
>   *2. find a group to share costs with*
>
> *conclusion:*

Linking ideas

You need to make sure that your reader can follow your ideas. In order to do this, each sentence should follow logically from the previous sentence and each paragraph should relate logically to the one before it. You can make sure your reader understands the relationship between the sentences and paragraphs in your essay by using 'marker' words and phrases.

Markers of Time Relationships

First ...	At this point ...	In the first stage/phase ...
Next, ...	After X ...	In the second stage/phase ...
Then ...	Finally, ...	In the final stage/phase ...

These are appropriate for describing a procedure where each step follows the previous one.

Markers of Main Points

Firstly, ...	Another X ...	One reason/advantage, ...
Secondly, ...	Furthermore, ...	Another reason/advantage ...
Thirdly, ...	In addition, ...	A further reason/advantage ...
Moreover, ...	The final reason/advantage ...	

These are appropriate for listing things such as reasons, advantages and disadvantages, risks and benefits.

Markers of Cause and Effect

As a result, ...	Due to ...
Consequently, ...	Because of ...
Therefore, ...	

Markers of Contrast and Comparison

Similarly, ...	In contrast, ...
In the same way, ...	On the other hand ...

You will find it useful to refer to the section 'Understanding Relationships in Passages' on page 17.

Writing a conclusion

Essays should not finish abruptly with the last main point. The final paragraph should provide a conclusion. The conclusion should give a sense of unity to your essay by making a general statement about the topic. In the IELTS, a short conclusion—perhaps only one or two sentences—is appropriate.

 EXAMPLE:

In conclusion, although there is some evidence for the role of physiology in determining the dominance of black athletes in some American sports, socio-logical factors appear more influential.

At this point, the procedure for copying from hard disk to diskette is complete.

Having completed this fourth stage, the final product—refined petroleum—has been obtained.

Provided the above recommendations are adopted, air-conditioning in hospitals is both safe and beneficial.

TASK 14

Write a conclusion for the following questions:

1. Write a report to your sponsoring agency describing the accommodation problems faced by foreign students in Britain. Make any necessary recommendations.

2. How far does a knowledge of statistics contribute to success in tertiary study?

3. Write a report for your sponsoring agency describing the English-language skills overseas students require. Make any recommendations you feel are necessary.

4. Should the same laws which prohibit the sale and consumption of heroin be applied to tobacco?

Writing-up 'procedures'

In the IELTS, the information which you need in order to describe a procedure may be given in the form of a table, diagram, or list.

In order to write up this kind of information, you should first underline the verbs.

 EXAMPLE:

AIRLINE SAFETY INSTRUCTIONS

Before take-off

<u>read</u> safety card in seat pocket

<u>check</u> location of emergency exits

<u>check</u> location of life jackets

During the flight

<u>keep</u> seat belts fastened at all times

do not <u>leave</u> hand luggage in aisles

In emergencies

If aircraft decompresses

<u>extinguish</u> cigarettes

<u>place</u> oxygen mask over mouth and nose

In the event of an emergency landing

<u>remove</u> shoes

<u>place</u> head on knees

<u>place</u> hands over head

<u>await</u> instructions

After underlining the verbs, you should then find subjects for them. Note that several alternative subjects may be possible. In the first example below, the verb 'read' could have three alternative subjects: 'the safety card', 'you' or 'passengers'.

 EXAMPLES:

Verbs	*Possible Subjects*
read	the safety card/you/passengers
check	location of emergency exits/you/passengers
check	location of life jacket/you/passengers
keep (fastened)	seat belts/you/passengers
(not)leave	hand luggage/you/passengers
extinguish	cigarettes/you/passengers
place	oxygen mask/you/passengers
remove	shoes/you/passengers
place	head/you/passengers
place	hands/you/passengers
await	instructions/you/passengers

The subject you choose will determine whether you use the active or passive form of the verb.

EXAMPLES:

Passengers should read the safety card.

You should check the location of emergency exits.

Seat belts should be kept fastened at all times.

TASK 15

Choose subjects for the verbs in the Airline Safety Instructions on page 77 and write complete sentences.

When writing up a procedure, you should remember to use appropriate markers in order to link the stages of the procedure. Compare the sample answer below with the list of Airline Safety instructions on page 77.

Sample Answer:

It is essential that passengers follow a number of regulations before and during flight and in the event of emergencies.

Before take-off, passengers should read the safety card in the seat pocket. They should also check the location of the emergency exits and the life jackets.

During the flight, seat belts should be kept fastened at all times when passengers are seated. Hand luggage must not be left in the aisles.

The following regulations apply in the case of emergencies. If the aircraft decompresses, cigarettes should be extinguished immediately and oxygen masks should be placed over the mouth and nose. In the event of an emergency landing, passengers should place their heads on their knees and their hands over their heads. They should then await instructions.

Failure to observe these instructions places all passengers at risk.

TASK 16*

Using the diagram on page 55, describe the procedure and equipment used to sort refuse for recycling. Write at least 150 words.

Points to remember in writing up

1. Contractions such as 'mustn't', 'can't', 'it'll', and 'haven't' are inappropriate in academic writing. In the IELTS test you should use uncontracted forms ('must not', 'cannot', etc.).

2. IELTS writing tasks require you to write complete sentences and paragraphs. You

must not write a list of numbered points, as in the following example concerning safety procedures for airline passengers:

Before take-off passengers should:

a. read the safety card

b. check the location of the emergency exits

c. check the location of the life jackets

3. Avoid personalising your language. For example instead of writing "I think air conditioning is a problem" simply write "Air conditioning is a problem." In describing processes, the passive can be used to create a more impersonal style which avoids references to people. For example, the sentence "You should always lock all doors before leaving home." looks more academic when the reference to "you" is eliminated when the passive is used: "All doors should be locked before leaving home."

4. If your handwriting is large, you may find there is not enough space to write the minimum number of words. Practise writing the required number of words in the space provided in the Sample Tests, remembering to begin each paragraph on a new line.

5. Examiners may unconsciously be influenced by the presentation of the writing, just as lecturers and tutors often are when they assess academic writing. Write as neatly and clearly as possible.

STAGE 5: CHECKING YOUR WRITING

This final stage should take no longer than two minutes.

Make sure you check your spelling and grammar. Mistakes can often be corrected by quickly checking through after you have finished writing. If you are in doubt about the spelling of a word or the accuracy of your grammar, try to choose a synonym or grammatical structure which you know is correct. The Diagnostic Tests on pages 88 to 93 will help you to identify weaknesses you may have in grammar and spelling. You should pay particular attention to those areas when checking your writing.

Your writing paper is sent to professional markers. Their objective is to assess whether you have fulfilled the requirements of the task. More specifically, they will consider the following five questions about your writing:

▶ ASSESSING YOUR WRITING

Does the essay have an organised structure?

Is the writing relevant to the task? Does the essay directly respond to the task?

Is the vocabulary appropriate?

Do grammatical and spelling mistakes occur often and make the essay difficult to read?

Does the essay demonstrate the writer's ability to construct complex sentences?

The following section examines each of these questions in turn and contains a series of tasks designed to assist you in evaluating your own writing.

Q: Does the essay have an organised structure?

The following task places you in the position of an IELTS examiner, evaluating the organisation of candidates' essays.

TASK 17*

Read the following question, the accompanying diagram and the two answers below (Versions 1 and 2). Assess how effectively each version is organised. You will find it helpful to re-read pages 70 to 79 before making your assessment.

Your sponsoring agency requires you to describe the admissions procedure to Australian tertiary institutions for overseas candidates.

You should refer to the notes below.

Make sure your description is:

1. relevant to the question and   2. well organised.

You should write at least 150 words.

Admissions Procedure to Australian Tertiary Institutions for Overseas Candidates

| Obtain and return application form. | → | Include statements of academic and language qualifications | → | Successful candidates receive an acceptance advice form. |

ON ACCEPTANCE:

■ pay half-year fees.

■ apply for visa at local consulate:

■ travel to study destination.

■ enrol.

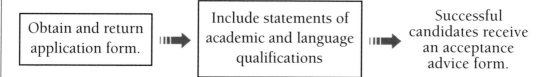

show acceptance advice form

have medical examination

pay overseas health-cover and visa fees

VERSION 1

Overseas candidates who wish to be admitted to an Australian tertiary institution require two documents: an acceptance advice form from the institution and a visa from an Australian consular office.

In order to do this, a candidate must first obtain, fill out and return an application form to the institution where he or she wishes to study. This form should include academic examination and English-language test results.

Successful applicants receive an acceptance advice form. On accepting the offer, the

continued on page 75

continued from page 74

candidate must pay fees for the first half-year and then apply for a visa from an Australian consular office.

Finally, after passing a medical examination, paying visa and overseas-student health-cover fees, the candidate may then travel to Australia.

At this point, the candidate has completed all of the required procedures and may then enrol.

VERSION 2

You have to fill our an application form. You should include academic and language test results. If you are successful you receive an acceptance advice form. If you decide to accept the offer you pay half-year fees. You should apply for a visa. You should take the acceptance advice form to a consular office, and have a medical examination. If you pass, you pay overseas-student health-cover and visa fees. You can travel to your study destination and enrol.

Q: Is the writing relevant to the task? Does the essay directly respond to the task?

Everything you write must be directly related to the question you are answering.

 EXAMPLES:

Versions 1 and 2 below were written by history students in the United Kingdom. They both answer the following question:

How did Indonesia gain its independence?

VERSION 1

Indonesia endured a long struggle against its colonial masters.

Nationalist groups, which had begun to form early in the 20th century, opposed Dutch colonial rule but were unable to obtain a negotiated independence.

The return of the Dutch after the defeat of the occupying Japanese was met with a newly strengthened resolve of the Indonesian nationalists, who unilaterally declared the independence of the nation.

After a fierce war, in which the Dutch were assisted by the British, the Indonesians emerged victorious. The Dutch withdrew and Indonesia was fully independent.

VERSION 2

Indonesia, which is the largest archipelago in the work, gained its independence from the Dutch in 1945.

Colonial exploitation, which had laster for hundreds of years, left the nation with numerous problems. The first decade after independence was characterised by attempts to establish suitable structures to provide the nation with adequate housing, education, and employment.

Like Version 1, Version 2 contains well-organised, accurate and interesting information. In contrast to Version 1, most of the information is not relevant to the question asked. The purpose of the question is to describe how Indonesian independence was gained. Therefore, the reference to 'the largest archipelago' in the first sentence is completely irrelevant. Equally irrelevant is the sentence: 'The first decade after independence was characterised by attempts to establish suitable structures to provide the nation with adequate housing, education, and employment.'

There is no limit to the kind of information you can include, provided that it is directly connected to the question. You should ask yourself before you write each sentence:

'How does this relate to the question?'

TASK 18*

The four sentences below appear in an answer to the following question:

> *What are the factors which contribute to air pollution? What recommendations would you make to improve the current situation?*

Which of the four sentences is/are irrelevant? Why?

A. The use of unleaded petrol, more efficient engines and modern exhaust-filtering devices can significantly reduce the emission of pollutants into the atmosphere.

B. In addition, funds must be allocated to develop sewage-treatment stations while the legislation prohibiting the unauthorised dumping of toxic wastes into the sea must be more adequately enforced.

C. Organic household refuse should be separated, prior to disposal, from non-organic matter. The householder should sort the non-organic waste, placing paper, plastics and glass into separate containers for future recycling.

D. The Greenhouse Effect can only be effectively reversed by a massive decrease in the emission of carbon dioxide into the atmosphere. This can largely be achieved by a reduction in the burning of fossil fuels and an end to large-scale deforestation.

TASK 19*

Versions 1 and 2 below are extracts from answers to the following question:

> *How effective are computers in teaching children to write?*

Assess the two versions for relevance.

VERSION 1

Word-processing packages enable learners to create texts, save and retrieve them,

continued on page 83

TASK 19* *continued from page 82*

insert or delete material. They often come with useful resources such as spell-checkers, dictionaries and thesauri.

Dedicated software is also available to teach basic writing skills such as sentence and paragraph formation. A study carried out at the University of Gatley found that learners learned basic skills more quickly when using dedicated software.

In addition, the computer can also create spreadsheets and may include a game package. Children are very fond of games. (Space Invaders is perhaps the most famous example.)

VERSION 2

Children generally enjoy playing computer games such as Space Invaders but often dislike learning how to write. 'Playing' with word-processing functions such as creating, inserting, deleting, saving and retrieving texts can motivate young learners to write.

Dedicated software is also available to teach basic sentence and paragraph construction. In a study carried out at the University of Gatley it was found that writing skills were learned more quickly when learners used dedicated software.

TASK 20*

Decide which of the versions below fails to answer the following question. Give reasons for your answer.

Explain how you would determine whether psychological characteristics are inherited or acquired.

VERSION 1

There are two experimental techniques which have been used to determine whether psychological characteristics are inherited or acquired.

The first technique involves the study of identical twins. Because they carry the same genetic information, they provide ideal subjects for observation in cases where they have been separated at birth and raised independently. By observing the psychological characteristics exhibited by a sufficiently large sample of adult identical twins separated at birth, it is then possible to find correlations in their psychological characteristics. These correlations can provide evidence to determine the inherited or acquired nature of psychological characteristics.

This latter technique has emerged as the major and most effective technique for deciding the heritability/acquisition debate in humans.

VERSION 2

Experiments have proved fairly conclusively that many psychological characteris-

continued on page 84

Task 20* *continued from page 83*

tics are inherited, and not acquired through environmental factors.

Heritability has been shown to be the dominant factor in lower mammals. Maternal behaviour can be induced in virgin female rats if they are injected with blood from rats which have recently given birth. The heritability/ acquisition issue is, however, not so easily solved, as it may not be applicable to human beings.

Observation of adult identical twins seems to provide conclusive evidence that many psychological characteristics are indeed inherited, rather than acquired. Identical adult twins who have been separated at birth and raised independently have been observed to exhibit the same psychological characteristics, such as alcoholism, despite different environmental influences. This strongly suggests that such characteristics are inherited. Environment does, however, still play an important part in the formation of personality. Not all the offspring of alcoholic parents become alcoholics; nor, conversely, do all alcoholics have alcoholic parents.

Nevertheless, research indicates that the major factor in the development of psychological characteristics is heritability, and not environment.

Q: Is the vocabulary appropriate?

 EXAMPLES:

Versions 1 and 2 below both answer the following question:

> *Describe the short- and long-term environmental effects of the deforestation of the Amazon Basin.*

What is the difference between the vocabulary of the two versions? Which version is more appropriate for a tertiary-level essay? Why?

VERSION 1

If you destroy the trees of the Amazon Basin, you create problems both now and in the future. In the short term, if people burn and log the forests, they may eliminate many types of flowers and animals. If the forest is removed, this takes away the food sources of the people who live there and who hunt and gather in them. After the protective canopy is removed, the delicate soils of the area may be rapidly eroded by the heavy rainfall. The people who clear the forests to raise animals and grow crops then find that the soil is useless.

Destroying trees does not just affect the Amazon Basin. It has the effects throughout the world. When millions of trees are lost, this decreases the earth's ability to remove carbon dioxide from the atmosphere and therefore builds up the quantity of Greenhouse gases. Also, if people burn the forests instead of just logging them, this increases the quantity of carbon dioxide in the atmosphere and makes the problem worse.

The deforestation of the Amazon Basin leads to the creation of both short-term and long-term problems. In the short term, burning and logging of the forests may eliminate many species of flora and fauna. The removal of forest also deprives forest hunting-and-gathering communities of food sources. After the removal of the protective canopy, the delicate soils of the area may be rapidly eroded by the heavy rainfall, thus making the land useless for the pastoral or arable activities which often accompany forest clearance.

The effects of such large-scale deforestation are not simply local, but also global. The loss of millions of tress decreases the earth's ability to remove carbon dioxide from the atmosphere, hence increasing the build-up of Greenhouse gases. Moreover, burning rather than mere logging actually leads to an increase in the quantity of carbon dioxide in the atmosphere, further worsening the problem.

Both versions provide the same information, but Version 2 is more appropriate as an academic essay. In this version, the events and activities described are more often expressed as nouns ('deforestation', 'creation', 'removal'). This is typical of written academic language. In Version 1, on the other hand, the actions are more often expressed through verbs ('destroy (the trees)', 'create', 'is removed'). This is more characteristic of informal spoken language and hence less appropriate in academic writing.

In order to 'translate' Version 1 into the more academically appropriate Version 2, you should:

> change the verbs into nouns or 'verb + ing' and eliminate, where possible, references to 'you', 'people' and other human agents;

> substitute expressions associated with informal spoken English with more 'academic' phrases.

Version 1: If you destroy the trees in the Amazon Basin, you create problems both now and in the future.

Version 2: The deforestation of the Amazon Basin leads to the creation of both short-term and long-term problems.

Note also that the writer of Version 2 has chosen academic terms, such as 'deforestation', 'Flora and fauna', 'global', 'pastoral and arable', 'hence'. As part of your study program you should make lists of the particular terms associated with your own discipline. You will find this helpful when you are writing assignments in tertiary study.

TASK 21

Identify examples of other such differences in vocabulary and structure in Versions 1 and 2 above.

Q: Do grammatical and spelling mistakes occur often and make the essay difficult to-read?

In assessing the accuracy of your grammar and spelling, you need as much objective feedback as possible. To identify areas of weakness you should ask teachers and native speakers of English to check your writing. Textbooks with answer keys can also be used. Your goal is to become more aware of those aspects of English grammar and spelling in which you consistently make mistakes. The Diagnostic Tests on pages 88 to 93 are designed to assist this process of self-assessment.

Q: Does the essay demonstrate the writer's ability to construct complex sentences?

Your ability to use longer, more complex sentences provides IELTS examiners with evidence of your grammatical proficiency.

  EXAMPLES:

VERSION 1

Between 1919 and 1933 there were free elections in Germany. Hitler came to power in 1933. From then until 1947 there were no free elections in Germany. There were no free elections in the German Democratic Republic (East Germany) until 1990. These took place after the fall of the communist regime. The former Communist Party was discredited. It still managed to gain a significant percentage of the vote

---
VERSION 2

Free elections were held in Germany between 1919 and 1933, the year in which Hitler came to power, but were not held again until 1947. In the former German Democratic Republic (East Germany), the first free elections only took place after the collapse of the communist regime. Even though the former Communist Party had been discredited, it still managed to gain a significant percentage of the vote.

Although both versions contain the same information, the writer of the second version has combined the seven sentences of Version 1 into three complex sentences. While both writers may have the same English-language competence, the second writer has demonstrated an ability to combine ideas into more complex structures and would score higher in the IELTS test.

The Diagnostic Tests on pages 88 to 93 will help you to assess your ability to form complex sentences accurately.

TASK 24*

Read the following writing task 2 question and the three answers (Essays A, B and C) which follow, considering their organisation, relevance, vocabulary and spelling.

The benefits of computers to modern society far outweigh the disadvantages. Discuss.

ESSAY A

The benefits of computer is more than its dissadvantages. The usage of computer in home, orgainizations showed is good for everybody.

First benefit computer is jobs. They do many jobs and the will be no necessary for more labour. This point will make less cost of production.

Next benefit of computers is better services which they give govement agencies. Healthe care and business are a good examples of this benefit. We have better service easier and faster form them and the same situation in health care.

But we must also remembering the potential dangers that computers affect.

The benefits of computers is more than it's disadvantages. The usage of computer in home and publick orgainisations as mentioned outweights the dissadvintages.

ESSAY B

Modern society has relied on computers very greatly. The computer has played an important role to change modern society in various ways. One of the positive effects of computer is doing dangerous works instead of human. For example, in computerised car assembly company computerised robots can do hard and dangerous works without discontinuation. In addition, computer has improved the speed of data processing. Data are very important to scientists and if there are not computers we could not develop out modern technology. We can go to the moon because computer caluculate the orbit of spaceship and timing of fuel injection and so on. Moreover, we can do shopping, book airplane and book theatre ticket at our home instead of going there.

However, computer can be used in many inadequate ways. For example, the

continued on page 88

Task 24* *continued from page 87*

privacy problem; somebody leaks other people's information on purpose. And nowadays, the personal computer, there are too many violent computer games, which has bad effects on children. Furthermore, many people lose their jobs because computer can shorten some process in the factory so that there are few people needed to control the factory.

As a result, computerised factory, data processing, mass communication are effected by computers in various ways so more many people are rely on computers.

ESSAY C

There have been two controversial issues about using computers in modern times. One issue states that using computers makes everyday life more easier and it must be wildly used. Antouer issue, in contrast to the first one, believes that computers has many disadvantages and therefore it should not be used at all. It is a matter of choice, to choose first issue or the second one.

Those who support using computers in everyday life usually mention the benefits of computers on the job, or at home or maybe as consumers. For example, on the job, we usually do our work much more faster if we use a computer; at home we can contact library or many other resources area that we need to get information by using computer and also consumers can use computer in order to do their work faster. Therefore it is useful to use computer widly around the world.

Another issue proclaims that using computer cause loss of jobs for many people and also losing the privacy of individuals. These machines can do multi-jobs at the same time without any need for people to help. Losing privacy is another main important disadvantage. Because any professional person in using computers may easily reach the personal information of the individuals due to lack of security system.

In conclusion it is necessary to use computer and do something about it's disadvantages. I do believe that, as the time passes, the technology of computers can reach to a point to overcomes to it's deficiencies and solve those problems that mentioned so far.

▶ DIAGNOSTIC TESTS

Test 1*: Grammar

Complete the following sentences by circling the missing words.

1. Science still _____ a cure for cancer.
   a. doesn't find
   b. haven't found
   c. hasn't found
   d. aren't finding

2. While he _____ a route to the Indies, Columbus discovered America.
   a. searched
   b. was discovering
   c. had searched for
   d. was searching for

3. Existing reserves of fossil fuel by _____ 2045.
   a. have been run out   c. is going to be run out
   b. will have run out   d. have run out

4. If logging of tropical rainforests continues at the present rate, _____ a 30 per cent increase in atmospheric CO2 by the year 2000.
   a. there will be   c. there would be
   b. there might have been   d. there could not have been

5. Only by investing heavily in value-added exports _____ from the present trade imbalance.
   a. the country can emerge   c. can the country emerge
   b. the country might emerge   d. the country emerged

6. The mystery of the double helix _____ , the scope for genetic engineering dramatically increased.
   a. having solved   c. solving
   b. having been solved   d. solved

7. since the mid-'60s considerable research in embryo transplants _____ .
   a. has carried out   c. has been carried out
   b. was done   d. was carried out

8. _____ several hypotheses have been advanced for the disappearance of the dinosaur, no conclusive evidence supports any of them.
   a. despite   c. although
   b. in spite of   d. in spite of the fact

9. Until the 16th century the earth _____ to be flat.
   a. is believed   c. believed
   b. has been believed   d. was believed

10. If the temperature of the reactor _____ 500°C higher meltdown would have occurred.
    a. was   c. was being
    b. had been   d. had

11. _____ adequate precautions are taken, there is no risk involved in the operation.
    a. Although   c. Nevertheless
    b. Providing   d. Even

12. My supervisor advised me to _____ the problem.
    a. look ahead   c. look out of
    b. look down   d. look into

13. The more acid you add to the solution, _____ it becomes.
    a. cloudier   c. the cloudiest
    b. the cloudier   d. more cloudy

14. The lecturer said 'It's time you _____ the literature review.'
    a. began   c. should begin
    b. begin   d. are beginning

15. After studying our experimental results, the tutor suggested _____ the experiment.
    a. us to repeat
    b. that we to repeat
    c. we repeat
    d. me to repeat

16. After _____ your results you should make an appointment with your tutor.
    a. you receiving
    b. you would have received
    c. you have received
    d. you received

17. You _____ the experiment twice, not once.
    a. should have carried out
    b. shouldn't have carried out
    c. haven't carried out
    d. couldn't have carried out

18. It looks _____ you've made a mistake.
    a. as
    b. as though
    c. if
    d. perhaps

19. After receiving her results, the student stopped _____ .
    a. to worry
    b. having worried
    c. worrying
    d. to be worried

20. You _____ include this section. It's not necessary
    a. must
    b. couldn't
    c. don't need
    d. don't have to

21. Unless _____ an extension at least one week before the due date, it will not be given.
    a. you request
    b. you will request
    c. you requested
    d. requesting

22. The assignment made me _____ .
    a. to think hard
    b. thinking hard
    c. think hard
    d. thought hard

23. The scientists were prohibited _____ the danger zone.
    a. to enter
    b. entering
    c. enter
    d. from entering

24. _____ the right answer I would have got full marks.
    a. Had I known
    b. If I would have known
    c. If I'll know
    d. If I was knowing

25. The results were _____ convincing that we decided to publish them.
    a. so
    b. such
    c. very
    d. so much

26. _____ way you do it, the answer is always the same.
    a. However
    b. Whichever
    c. Who ever
    d. Why ever

27. _____ producing methane, the process also produces carbon monoxide.
    a. Apart
    b. As well
    c. Besides
    d. In addition

28. The biologist admitted _____ excessive numbers of animals in
    laboratory tests.
    a. using   c. being used
    b. to use   d. used

29. A whale is a mammal, _____ it is warm-blooded and gives milk to its young.
    a. who   c. which means that
    b. which   d. that

30. He appears _____ minor problems.
    a. to have had   c. was having
    b. having   d. had

31. The books _____ are very interesting.
    a. which we have read them   c. which we read them
    b. we have read   d. whose we have read

32. Einstein, _____ changed our way of seeing the universe, did not learn to read
    until he was ten.
    a. which theories   c. whose theories
    b. that his theories   d. who theories

33. Students _____ that course always enjoy it.
    a. who taking   c. which take
    b. take   d. who take

34. The liquid _____ by a compressed-air blast.
    a. is extracted   c. extracted
    b. extracts   d. is extracting

35. The problems facing the scientists were _____ than they had expected.
    a. biggest   c. very bigger
    b. much bigger   d. very big

Test 2*: Sentence Construction

By using the words in brackets, join each of the following pairs of sentences to form one
sentence. You may need to change some of the words.

☞   EXAMPLES:

      He bought a laptop computer. His friend advised him against it. (in spite of)

      Sample answer: He bought a laptop computer in spite of his friend advising
                 him against it.

1. The results of the experiment were successful. The government cut the funding.
   (although)

2. She chose to study accounting. Accounting has good employment prospects.
   (because of)

3. The tree guard concentrates precipitation around the root system. It also protects
   against animal foraging. (as well as)

4. In-vitro fertilisation has brought joy to childless couples. It has also created legal dilemmas. (not only/but also)

5. The regulations concerning non-government schools have failed to address the real issues. The regulations were introduced in May this year. (which)

6. The liquid helium reaches the decompression chamber. It becomes a gas. (as soon as)

7. Breakthroughs in fibre-optic technology have taken place. This has enabled enormous improvements in infrastructural development. (resulted from)

8. She wrote very slowly. She did not finish the Writing section. (if)

9. The 'fellow servant rule' effectively subsidised the industrial revolution. It denied workers compensation for industrial accidents. (by)

10. A significant diminution in the size of the coral reef occurred. This was caused by a proliferation of the Crown of Thorns, a starfish which feeds on coral polyps. (as a result)

Test 3*: Spelling

The following list contains 200 words commonly found in academic writing. Eighty of these words are spelt incorrectly. Locate and correct the incorrectly spelt words.

theory	fasilities	psichological	weakness	corelation
thesis	benefits	abstract	strengths	materiel
superviser	apropriate	concreet	apparartus	dramatically
lecturar	knowlege	crytisism	approximatly	phase
tutor	responsability	appendices	measurment	discusion
seminar	attitude	persuit	statistical	concern
governement	investigation	questionaire	decreese	emfasise
department	resourse	performance	activate	efficency
sektion	hierarchy	comparitive	conventional	design
examenation	experriment	relatively	immersion	depletion
proposel	determine	significant	stabilisation	continuous
justification	implication	sustanable	seqential	simulator
contrery	charactarise	systematically	elementery	variabillity
justify	gradualy	eqipment	simultanous	sample
oposite	research	standard	findings	assessment
feature	technique	literature	influence	per capita
conclusion	effectiveness	awareness	outcome	orientation
sistem	laboratory	programming	frequently	riview
inferr	comprehensive	yield	configuration	involvment
divided	contradiction	approches	inevitabally	consumtion
objective	paralel	analytical	specification	consider
analisys	especially	application	predominently	abundence
hypothesis	methodology	planning	comparison	future
development	challenge	further	minor	relationship

beleif	sinthesise	moddification	observe	specify
teoretical	quote	distrebution	opinion	polisy
emission	concentration	conditions	attemt	produce
quantitative	achievment	describe	perspectife	responce
allocation	operate	details	expect	ensure
graphik	position	structure	select	edit
distribute	excede	provide	exclude	patern
bibliography	surpass	conduct	multipel	employ
significanse	fluctuation	report	establish	redundant
serve	fraimwork	essay	adopt	irrelevant
recegnise	crucial	assinement	assume	depth
role	predict	differ	diverse	match
limitation	outline	affect	estimete	correspond
maxamise	progres	seperate	vary	factor
sumarise	cronological	recieve	lengthen	author
consistency	specific	enable	paramater	aquire

▶ **FURTHER STUDY**

The writing tasks in IELTS parallel the kinds of written tasks you may have to do in tertiary study. How much do you know about tertiary writing tasks?

TASK 25

Before beginning tertiary study, it is useful to find out what you will be required to write in your future courses. You can do this by contacting course conveners or departmental offices. Ask if it is possible to obtain lists of writing assignments for the coming academic session or for past years. You can provide them with a check list to see how many types of text are required. For example, do you have to write:

Summaries of articles or books?	Laboratory notes?
Experimental or research reports?	Essays?
Tutorial papers?	Examination essays or short answers?
Tables, graphs, diagrams?	Annotated bibliographies?
Literature reviews?	Position papers?
Theses?	Computer programs?

When you have identified the kinds of texts you will be required to write, you should try to obtain examples so that you can familiarise yourself with their characteristics. The materials for further study listed at the end of this unit will provide you with a starting point for this research.

The following writing tasks are designed to give you further practice in IELTS writing. In order to simulate test conditions you should complete the tasks in the recommended time without the aid of a dictionary.

Practice Questions for General Training Module Candidates

You have had an accident and are in hospital. Write a letter to your college administration explaining why you will be absent from class for the next month. Ask for advice about how to continue your studies during this period. (20 minutes)

You find that your study load is too heavy. Write a letter to your college teacher explaining why you need to withdraw from two courses. Ask if it is possible to obtain a refund. (20 minutes)

Write a report for your college teacher describing an English-language course which you have taken. Explain why it is not necessary for you to take further English-language courses. (40 minutes)

You want to apply for the following job. Write a letter to Mr Moore describing your previous experience and explaining why you would be suitable for the job. (20 minutes)

> Waiter/waitress required for evening work. Some experience necessary. Write to: Mr K. Moore, Cafe Royale.

You are writing your first letter to a 'pen pal'. Describe your previous studies and work experience, your current activities, hobbies and interests. Tell your pen pal that you will be visiting his/her country during the summer vacation and suggest meeting him/her. (20 minutes)

Practice Questions for Academic Module Candidates

What are the language skills required by students at tertiary institutions? (40 minutes)

To what extent should university courses be geared to the economic needs of society? (40 minutes)

What are the critical test-taking strategies that candidates should use in the IELTS Writing section? In your answer, refer to the notes on page 95. (20 minutes)

Some old people live with their sons and daughters, others in special homes with other old people. In your opinion, who should be responsible for the elderly?

In many countries military service is compulsory for young people. What is the case for and against abolishing compulsory military service?

It has been argued that nuclear weapons have created a safer world and prevented another world war. Is the world really a safer place because of them?

► TEST-TAKING STRATEGIES

Read the task instructions carefully, checking that you understand the audience, topic, purpose, and requirements.

Use the information sources required by the task.

Take time to make notes and plan an outline.

Follow the time recommendations carefully.

During all stages keep assessment criteria in mind.

► MATERIALS FOR FURTHER STUDY

You may find the following books useful:

Benesch, S. et al. 1987. *Academic Writing Workshop*. Belmont, California: Wadsworth.

Benesch, S. and B. Rorschach. 1989. *Academic Writing Workshop II*. Belmont, California: Wadsworth.

Dudley-Evans, T. 1985. *Writing Laboratory Reports*. Melbourne: Nelson.

Hamp-Lyons, L. and B. Heasley. 1987. *Study Writing: A Course in Written English for Academic and Professional Purposes*. Cambridge: Cambridge University Press.

Hartfiel, V.F. et al. 1985. *Learning E.S.L. Composition*. Cambridge: Newbury House.

McEvedy, M.R. et al. 1990. *Read, Note, Write; How to Prepare Assignments*. South Melbourne: Nelson.

Oshima, A. and A. Hogue. 1983. *Writing Academic English*. Reading, Mass.: Addison-Wesley.

Pack, A.C. and L.E. Henrichsen. 1980. *Sentence Combination. Writing and Combining Standard English Sentences*. Cambridge: Newbury House.

Rajagopalan, R. 1990. *Writing Laboratory and Workshop Reports*. Jurong Town, Singapore: Longman.

Weissberg, R. and S. Buker. 1990. *Writing Up Research: Report Writing for Students of English*. Englewood Cliffs, N.J.: Prentice Hall Regents.

GRAMMAR BOOKS

Leech, G. and J. Svartvik. 1975. *A Communicative Grammar of English*. Harlow: Longman.

Murphy, R. 1985. *English Grammar in Use: A Self-Study Guide*. Cambridge: Cambridge University Press.

Swan, M. 1981. *Practical English Usage*. Oxford: Oxford University Press.

IELTS: STRATEGIES FOR STUDY

▶ UNIT 3 *Listening*

This unit contains

'The Listening section was definitely the most difficult for me. We only heard the tapes once and some of the speakers seemed to talk as fast as rockets. I was trying to read the questions, listen to the tape and write the answers all at the same time. I couldn't understand a few things, got very confused and only managed to write a quarter of the answers.

Korean IELTS candidate

Many other test candidates experience similar difficulties in the Listening section. This unit explores these difficulties and suggests strategies for overcoming them.

▶ LISTENING TEST DESCRIPTION

The Listening Test lasts 40 minutes and generally contains four sections. You will hear the listening passages on a cassette tape. All instructions are also given on tape, not by the examiner in the room.

The sections of the Listening Test are generally structured as follows. They contain either one longer passage lasting about five minutes or a series of short, linked passages, each lasting about one minute. Before each section, candidates are given 30 seconds to study the tasks in that section. Each passage is played only once and candidates are required to write their answers while they are listening. At the end of each section, candidates are given 30 seconds to check their answers. At the end of the test, candidates are given ten minutes to check all their answers and write them up on a special answer sheet.

GENERAL TRAINING MODULE

Candidates for the General Training Module take the same Listening Test as all other candidates.

▶ ANTICIPATING WHAT YOU WILL HEAR

Many people believe that listening effectively simply means understanding all the words they hear. They are therefore convinced that if they do not understand every word, they will not be able to answer the test questions. This is incorrect.

Even when listening to our native languages, we do not always understand every word, for example in a noisy room or on a bad telephone connection. In these situations, we instinctively use anticipating and guessing strategies to understand the message. Think about what you do, for example, when you receive a telephone call. What kinds of things do you try to anticipate when the phone starts ringing and then when the caller starts speaking?

Because of the increased difficulties you face when listening to a foreign language, it is important to become conscious of the instinctive strategies you already use.

IELTS: STRATEGIES FOR STUDY

The key strategy in the IELTS Listening section is to anticipate what you are going to hear. In your study program, you need to anticipate the kinds of situations you are likely to hear and in the test itself you must anticipate the information you need to get from the passages. Candidates who fail to do this (such as the candidate quoted at the beginning of this unit) are unable to carry out the tasks and score badly.

ANTICIPATING IELTS LISTENING SITUATIONS

IELTS listening passages reflect common situations which you might experience when living and studying in an English-speaking country.

 EXAMPLE:

meeting an English-speaking passenger on your flight towards your study destination

answering the questions of customs/passport officials at the airport

checking into a student residential college

asking a passer-by for directions to the nearest bank/post office, etc.

making an appointment to meet a friend

enrolling at the International Students' Office

listening to the radio news/weather forecast

attending a library orientation talk

attending your first college or university class

All these situations can be divided into two types:

- social survival situations;
- study-related situations.

TASK 1

Extend the list of examples as much as you can by finding examples of both basic types of situation. To help you focus on the situations you might meet in the IELTS Listening section, think about what you will do from the moment you arrive in the country where you will study to the moment you leave your first class or lecture.

Suggestions:
If you are already living in an English-speaking country, include as many of the situations as you can that you have already encountered. If you are not living in an English-speaking country, try to talk to people from your own country who have already studied abroad. Ask them to remember as much as they can about their first few weeks after arrival.

continued on page 100

continued from page 99

Who did they speak to when travelling to their study destination?

How did they travel from the airport to the town or city where they were going to live?

How did they find accommodation?

How much contact did they have with native English speakers?

Did they have any difficulty in understanding their teachers?

Which listening situations did they find most difficult?

Contact the International Students' Office of the institutions where you are interested in studying. Ask them for information about what you are likely to encounter when you arrive at your destination.

Will you be met by a university official at the airport? (If so, will that person speak your language? How will you travel from the airport to the city?)

Where will you stay when you arrive?

Is there an orientation week at your institution? If so, what is involved?

What bureaucratic procedures will you have to carry out? How, for example, do you get medical assistance?

Is it possible to obtain work on/off campus?

Do you have to choose optional courses? If so, what information is available to help you make your choice? Is there an academic adviser?

Contact the heads of departments of the institutions where you are considering studying. You can write or, if you are already living in the same city, you can telephone to make an appointment to see them. This is a normal procedure in tertiary education and teachers are generally helpful and informative. Find out as much as you can about the kinds of listening situation you will encounter. In some institutions, tapes of lectures may also be available for you to borrow. If you are already living in the country where you plan to study, you can ask the institution if it is possible to attend lectures and tutorials before commencing your course.

LISTENING FOR INFORMATION

So far you have been concentrating on what you will be listening to – that is, the kinds of situations you might hear. You also need to make predictions about what you will be listening for – the specific information you need to focus on as a listener. If you have a specific focus, then you do not need to understand everything you hear. As in reading, this focus enables you to locate information more efficiently.

EXAMPLE:

Your supervisor is telling you what she requires in your next written assignment.

In this situation, you would probably listen for the following specific information: the topic and purpose of the assignment, the required length, recommended reading, the date when the assignment should be handed in.

TASK 2*

What information would you listen for in the following situations?

1. The Overseas Students' Officer at your college is explaining arrangements for a coach trip into the country which you would like to go on.

2. A university lecture.

3. The college librarian is introducing first-year students to the library.

4. You have heard the news headlines on the radio. An oil tanker has sunk.

5. You are listening to a telephone conversation between a student who wants to rent a flat and the owner of the flat.

In the IELTS test, the questions themselves will determine what you have to listen for. Remember: you listen to everything on the tape, but you only listen for specific points of information.

▶ LISTENING TASK INSTRUCTIONS

The basic format of test instructions is as follows:

At the beginning of each section, the speaker on the tape gives a brief introduction to the situation.

 EXAMPLE:

'Ahmad, a student from Algeria, is arriving at the airport. Waiting for him are his hosts, Mr and Mrs Johnson.'

The speaker then gives instructions.

 EXAMPLE:

'Read questions 7 to 13. As you listen to the tape, write the correct answer in the spaces provided. You will hear the tape once only, so you should answer the questions as you listen. You have 30 seconds to study the questions. '

During the 30 seconds you need to:

- study the questions and make sure you understand them
- decide what to listen for
- make sure you know where to write your answers.

After 30 seconds the speaker repeats the numbers of the questions you have to answer. Then the passage begins.

▶ LISTENING STRATEGIES

The following sample tasks introduce a range of strategies that will help you to respond to questions rapidly and effectively.

SAMPLE TASK 1: an example of a picture-based task containing four short listening passages.

You hear the speaker say:

'Liz is phoning Michael. She wants to arrange to meet him tonight. Decide which of the pictures best fits what you hear on the tape, and circle the letter under that picture.'

On the test paper you see the following questions:

1. What do they decide to do?

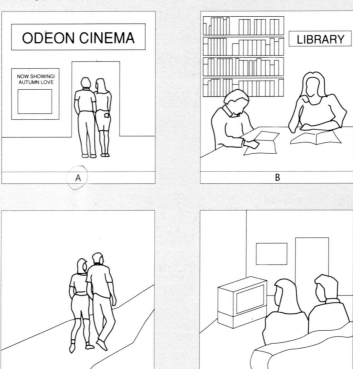

continued on page 103

SAMPLE TASK 1: *continued from page 102*

2. Where is the cinema?

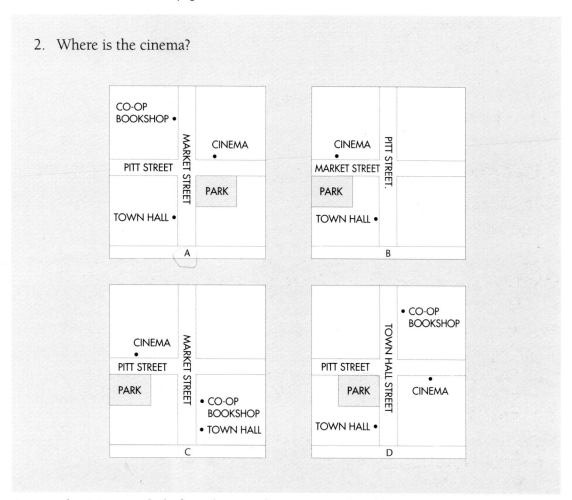

During the 30 seconds before the tape begins, you should match the questions to the pictures, 'translating' them into words. In Question 1, for example, 'What do they decide to do?' = 'Do they decide to go to the cinema?/study at the library?/see a film?/go for a walk?/watch TV at home?'. By translating in this way, you can anticipate the key vocabulary. In Question 2, for example, you should anticipate directions ('turn left/right', 'it's opposite/in front of/on the corner', etc.)

TASK 3*

Use these strategies for Question 3 on the next page.

3. How is Michael going to get there?

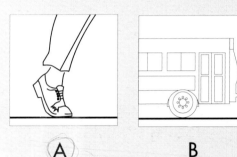 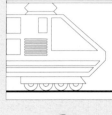 

| A | B | C | D |

TASK 4*

Listen to Tape Exercise 1 once only and answer questions 1–3.

SAMPLE TASK 2: an example of a form-filling task.

The speaker says:

> 'Gerharde has just moved to a new area of town and wants to join the local library. A librarian is filling in an application form, asking Gerharde for details. Look at questions 4 to 7.'

On the test paper you see:

APPLICATION FORM

Name (4) Gerharde Esterhazy

Date of birth (5) 7/12/1959

Address (6) 13 albion Street, Leichhardt 2046

Phone number (7) 5674990

To prepare for this passage, you should read the questions and decide what you need to listen for. Remember that the information you hear on the tape may be expressed differently from the words which you see on the form. The librarian, for example, may ask: 'Could you tell me when you were born?', which gives you the information you need to fill in 'Date of birth'.

TASK 5*

Anticipate how the information about 'address' might be asked on the tape.

In form-filling tasks you should also be ready to listen for numbers and letters. In this task, for example, you can see from the form that you will have to listen for numbers (in 5,6,7,) and names (4 and 6).

TASK 6*

Listen to Tape Exercise 2 once only and answer questions 4 to 7.

Understanding numbers is an important part of academic listening and may be assessed in the IELTS test. You should be familiar with the following conventions:

Telephone numbers:
These are usually spoken as individual numbers. Example: 276938 = 'two seven six nine three eight'. With seven-digit numbers, speakers often divide them into one group of three and one group of four, with a short pause between the groups. Example: 625 4598 = 'six two five...four five nine eight'.

Sometimes a few numbers are grouped into a larger number, especially when this involves consecutive zeros. Example: 979 6000 = 'nine seven nine six thousand'.

In British and Australian English, '0' in telephone numbers is spoken as the letter 'o', as in 'go'.

Sometimes the words 'double' and 'triple' are used. Example: 224 6555 = 'double two four:... six triple five'.

Decimal numbers:

Decimal numbers are introduced with the word 'point' and then each decimal number is spoken individually. Example: 14.73 = 'fourteen point seven three'.

When talking about prices, the word 'point' is not usually used. The decimal numbers are usually combined. Example: $12.45 = 'twelve dollars (and) forty-five (cents)'. The name of the currency is often left out too = 'twelve forty-five'.

Fractions:

With the exception of 'a half', 'quarter(s)', and 'third(s)', fractions are expressed as '... ths'. Example: ⅞ = 'seven-eighths', ‰ = 'nine-tenths'.

Thousands:

Apart from the standard system, in which, for example, 1500 = 'one thousand five hundred', it is also possible to express thousands as the equivalent number of hundreds. Examples: 1500 = 'fifteen hundred'; 2700 = 'twenty-seven hundred', 1123 = 'eleven hundred and twenty-three'. This system is quite common in talking about prices.

If you are intending to study a subject which involves mathematics you need to know more specialised terms such as 'square root', 'squared', 'cubed', 'x to the power y' and Greek letters such as 'chi', 'sigma', and 'pi' which may be pronounced differently in English to the way they are in your own language. These are too specialised to be tested in the IELTS test.

TASK 7*

Listen to Tape Exercise 3 once only and write down the numbers you hear.

Candidates who are not familiar with the pronunciation of the alphabet in English may encounter difficulties in tasks which involve spelling. You need to practise listening to the way in which native speakers of English spell words.

TASK 8*

Listen to Tape Exercise 4 once only and write down the letters you hear.

TASK 9*

Listen to Tape Exercise 5 and write down the personal names and place names you hear. When you check the answer key, identify which letters are a problem for you and work with a study partner to practise them.

SAMPLE TASK 3: an example of an information-matching task.

The speaker says:

Jaedok attends an orientation talk given by the Overseas Student Office at his university. As you listen to the recording, answer questions 8-16 by circling T for 'True' and F for 'False.' The first one has been done for you. First read questions 8-16.'

On the test paper you see the following:

8.	Students must enrol by January 25.	T	F
9.	All courses begin on March 6.	T	F
10.	Some students can obtain identity cards from the Undergraduate Studies Office.	T	F
11.	Students require a separate library borrowing card.	T	F
12.	In term time the Overseas Student Office is open until 6 p.m.	T	F
13.	The bank is open on Sundays.	T	F
14.	Students can sometimes cash cheques at the Overseas Student Office.	T	F
15.	The doctor sees patients only between Monday and Friday.	T	F
16.	If you want to use the gymnasium you must have a special membership card.	T	F

In answering true/false questions, there are three kinds of information you should focus on:

Words that limit nouns. In Question 10, for example, the noun 'students' is limited by the word 'some'. If the speaker says 'all students', then the statement is false.

Words that limit verbs. In Question 10, for example, the verb 'obtain' is limited by the word 'can'. If the speaker says 'must obtain', then the statement is again false.

The accuracy of facts. In Question 8, for example, the date given is January 25. If the speaker on the tape does not give the same date, then the statement is obviously false.

Before you hear the passage, you should try to identify and underline the parts of these statements which you need to listen for.

TASK 10*

Underline what you should listen for in Questions 11-16 above.

TASK 11*

Listen to Tape Exercise 6 once only and answer questions 8-16 on page 107.

SAMPLE TASK 4: an example of an open-question task.

The speaker says:

'Richard is interviewing an applicant for a job in the office where he works. He is asking the applicant about her experience at university. Listen to their conversation and answer Questions 17 to 25 by writing a word or a short phrase in the space provided. Now look at Questions 17 to 25.'

On the test paper you see the following:

17. Why did Sandy decide to study Psychology?

18. What did she enjoy most about her course?

19. What was her first job?

20. What aspect of her course did she find most relevant to her job?

21. Why did she leave her previous job?

22. Why did she apply for this job?

23. How did she find out about the vacancy?

24. Where did she learn to type?

25. What are her long-term goals?

Your answers:

17. great

18. _____

19. researcher

20. _____

21. She wants to chall

22. by friend

23. secretary course

24. ✓

25. teaching

In the 30 seconds before you hear the tape, you should study the questions as quickly as possible. If you do not know the meaning of some words, use surrounding words and other questions to guess the possible meaning. When you listen to the passage you will have more information to help you guess. In Question 23, for example, you may not know the meaning of the word 'vacancy'. You can, however, assume that it is a job-related word and you also know that it is something you can 'find out about.' When you listen to the tape you should be prepared to listen for information about how Sandy found out about some aspect of the job.

You should also try to anticipate possible answers. In Question 21, for example, you might anticipate that Sandy resigned from her last job because she was not satisfied with her salary or that the job was not interesting or challenging or that it was too far to travel to work, etc.

Remember that the information you are listening for may be expressed differently from the statements that you read on the test paper. The information needed to answer Question 19, for example, may be given in response to 'Where did you work after *graduating?*'.

TASK 12*

Anticipate what you need to listen for to answer Questions 22 to 25.

TASK 13*

Listen to Tape Exercise 7 once only and answer questions 17–25.

SAMPLE TASK 5: an example of a gap-filling task

The speaker says:

'Listen to this radio news item. Fill in the gaps numbered 26 to 34 by writing the missing words in the spaces below. First, read questions 26 to 34.'

On the test paper you see:

The Macquarie River has __26__ its banks, flooding the town of Stanton. All __27__ links to the town have been cut and the population of __28__ is now being supplied with medical supplies and __29__ by helicopter. At least two people were drowned when floodwaters trapped them in their __30__. Almost all of the town's inhabitants have lost their __31__ and are living in army __32__. For information about the disaster ring __33__. The Government has set up a relief fund. Contributions can be paid into the State Bank no __34__.

Your answers:

26.	31.
27.	32.
28.	33.
29.	34.
30.	

In order to answer gap-filling tasks like this, you should, before the tape is played, first look at the words before and after each gap and decide what kind of information is missing. You may be unable to finish in the 30 seconds, but make sure that you have studied at least the first four gaps and know where to write your answers.

By looking at the words surrounding gap 26, for example, you know that the missing word or phrase refers to what a river can do to its banks. You should anticipate words such as 'burst', 'overflow' or 'break'. Similarly, the words surrounding gap 29 help you to limit the range of possibilities to words such as 'assistance', 'clothing', food', 'shelter', etc.

TASK 14*

Anticipate possible answers for gaps 30 to 34.

Some candidates assume that the passage they read is a direct transcript of the taped passage and become confused when the words they hear on the tape are different. The passage you read is not a transcript of the passage you hear. It is only a summary of the main information. The actual taped text in this case is a news report in which the radio news reader introduces the story and then hands over to a reporter in the field who interviews witnesses.

You read (*extract*)

> The Macquarie River has __26__ its banks, flooding the town of Stanton. All __27__ links to the town have been cut and the population of __28__ is now being supplied with medical supplies and __29__ by helicopter.

You hear (*extract*)

> *'Emergency in the state's Northern District. The Macquarie River has burst its banks in the Northern District, flooding the town of Stanton about 300 kilometres north of the state capital. The Golden City and Macquarie Valley Highways – Stanton's only road links with the outside world – are now impassable. This small wheat-belt town with a population of 3000 is now entirely dependent for its survival on the efforts of the army's Disaster Intervention Squad which is bringing emergency medical supplies and food into the area by helicopter. Our correspondent Maxine Zenith flew into Stanton with the army.'*

TASK 15*

Listen to Tape Exercise 8 once only and answer questions 26–34 on page 109.

The requirement to read, listen and write in a very short time causes difficulty for some candidates. You need a lot of practice to improve your performance in this kind of task (see Exercises on page 117).

▶ UNDERSTANDING LECTURES AND TALKS

The strategies used in listening to lectures and seminar presentations are relevant to listening to IELTS talks, such as the orientation talk in Tape Exercise 6.

Before listening to a lecture or talk, you can do a lot to prepare yourself for what you will hear. If, for example, you know in advance that the subject of a lecture is 'the role of computers in education' then you can anticipate some of the language that you will hear by using your knowledge of the subject and by reading an introductory account of the subject.

While you are listening to a lecture or talk, you need to recognise when the speaker is carrying out functions such as:

- introducing a new topic
- introducing a main point
- giving an example
- giving instructions
- contrasting

- emphasising
- restating information in different ways
- giving irrelevant information
- making a summary

TASK 16*

Speakers often indicate these functions by using 'marker' phrases. Match the phrases in the left hand column to the descriptions in the right-hand column. Some functions correspond to more than one marker phrase.

1. introducing a new topic
2. emphasising a main point
3. giving an example
4. giving instructions
5. contrasting
6. restating information in different ways
7. giving irrelevant information
8. making a summary

a. 'what I mean by that is ...'
b. 'to put it another way ...'
c. 'so what we've got so far is ...'
d. I'm going to kick off by talking about . . . '
e. 'what you've got to realise is ...'
f. 'that reminds me of the time my husband and I ...'
g. 'the crux of the matter is ...'
h. 'as we've seen today ...'
i. 'in other words . . .'
j. 'this is not always the case ...'
k. 'the next thing we'll be looking at . . .'
l. 'there are three main concepts you should bear in mind ...'
m. 'however, you've got to remember. . .'

TASK 17*

You are going to listen to a lecture on 'global warming and its effects on coastal areas'. Before listening to the lecture, predict as much as you can about what you are going to hear. Then listen to Tape Exercise 9 once only and decide which of the following notes (A, B, C) contains all the main points of the lecture.

Question 9

A. *Read (for tute next week)*   *Henderson-Sellers and Blong (Greenhouse E.)*
                                    Pearman (review of issues in Australia)
                                    Lovelock (general introduction)

   Effects of sea-level rise (difficult to predict precise rise)

   1. Damage to infrastructure (roads, rail, etc).

   2. Shoreline retreat.

   3. Coastal flooding, n.b. Brisbane.

   4. Saltwater penetration, e.g. Myall Lakes (affects irrigation, drinking water).

   5. Tidal flooding.

B. *Australia has 12,000 kilometre coastline: range of natural disasters.*
   Greenhouse Effect, Henderson-Sellers and Blong, Lovelock and Pearman.

   1. 50 metre rise causes damage to ports, roads, rail links.

   2. Blue area on map indicates predicted flooding in Brisbane.

   3. Saltwater destroys freshwater ecosystems.

   4. Drinking water a problem.

C. *Many natural problems in Australia, e.g. floods, drought, cyclones.*

   *   Flooding of coastal structures.*

   *   Sea moves inland (e.g. Gulf of Carpentaria).*

   *   Beachfront apartments float away.*

   *   Myall Lakes will reconnect with the sea.*

   *   Cyclone Tracy Dec. 25, 1974.*

   *   Increased deposits cause shoreline to extend in some areas.*

TASK 18

Listen to the global-warming lecture (Tape Exercise 9) again and find examples of the marker phrases listed before.

▶ **TEST-TAKING STRATEGIES**

In each section, the information you need to answer one question comes before the information for the next question. There is no instruction, however, to move on to the next question: you must decide this yourself.

Difficulties occur when candidates are unable to find a correct answer. They may continue to focus on one question, waiting to hear the information that will help them to answer it. If they continue to wait, they may miss the information that will help them to answer the next questions. As a result, candidates may lose their place and panic.

To prevent this happening, you need to focus on at least **two** questions at all times.

   EXAMPLE:

You read (*extract*)

At exactly ....1.... this afternoon, the city of Harristown was struck by a violent ....2..... . It has now been confirmed that over ....3.... people have been killed and another 150 seriously injured.

You hear (*extract*)

'*The state of Queensland is still in shock tonight after the biggest natural disaster in Australian history. At precisely half past five this afternoon, at the height of the Harristown rush hour, the city was rocked by a devastating earthquake that registered 6.5 on the Richter scale. Now we cross over to our reporter Helen Pratt reporting from Harristown's devastated city centre.*'

'*I'm standing outside what was Harristown's town hall – now just a pile of rubble. At least 50 people are believed to have been trapped when the building collapsed this afternoon and rescue workers are at this moment fighting to find survivors under the rubble. So far more than 60 people have been confirmed dead and the figure is expected to rise. Reports from St Patrick's Hospital, itself severely damaged in the 'quake, indicate that a further 150 people have been admitted with serious injuries...*'

A candidate who focuses only on gap 1, waiting to hear the information about the time, may miss this information but continue to wait, hoping to hear it. By this point, the information for gaps 2 and 3 may have already passed. When the candidate moves on to gap 2, it is already too late to catch up.

In this example, candidates should focus on both gaps 1 and 2, anticipating that 1 refers to time and 2 to some kind of disaster. Even if they miss the information about time, they are anticipating gap 2 and are therefore able to respond when they hear the word 'earthquake'. As soon as they answer this question, they focus on the next two questions, waiting for information about the numbers of dead and injured.

The same strategy is essential in those sections which consist of two or more passages (see Sample Task 1 on page 102). There is no instruction to move from one question to the next. You need to look ahead and focus on two questions.

► FURTHER STUDY

Remember that you should attempt to answer every question. No penalties are given for incorrect answers.

In your study program you need to:

- find appropriate listening passages
- increase your confidence in listening
- practise the skills required by the IELTS test.

FINDING APPROPRIATE LISTENING PASSAGES

English-language radio programs are a useful source of appropriate listening passages: news broadcasts, talks, interviews, and dramatic dialogues. You can obtain program guides by writing to the following stations: BBC World Service, Radio Australia, Canadian Broadcasting Corporation, Voice of America. Station addresses can be supplied by the cultural centres or consulates of the respective countries.

For many of the tasks described below, it is useful to record the programs you listen to.

INCREASING YOUR CONFIDENCE IN LISTENING

Many people who listen to a foreign language think that the speakers of that language speak very quickly and 'eat their words'. Because they do not understand every word, they often feel that they are missing essential information. You need to get used to listening to English without feeling panic or frustration when you don't understand everything. Regular listening will improve your confidence in understanding English spoken at different speeds with different accents.

Learning to listen effectively does not mean simply listening. You must always have a focus. When listening to passages, ask yourself these focusing questions:

- What am I listening to? Is it, for example, a news item? An interview? A story?
- How many people are speaking?
- What is the topic?
- Are they reading a script, speaking from notes or speaking spontaneously?
- What are the speakers trying to do? To entertain? To explain? To describe?

If you can answer these questions you have completed the task. Do this exercise every day, listening for at least 25 minutes, the actual listening time of the IELTS test. As your study program progresses, you should practise more specific tasks as suggested in the section below. Remember it takes a long time to become as efficient a listener in a foreign language as you are in your own.

PRACTISING THE SKILLS REQUIRED BY THE IELTS TEST

Exercises for Independent Study

Exercise 1

Before listening to a passage, predict as much as you can about what you are going to hear. You can use radio program guides or the titles of passages in textbooks.

 EXAMPLE:

Radio Guide: Saturday, December 7

2.00–2 30	Antarctica: the next tourist destination? Interview with tour operator Georgia Pikios.
2.30–3.00	'My Favourite Music', featuring this week's celebrity guest Lady Ruth Lopert.
3.00	News and weather.

If you choose to listen to the 2.00 program, you might predict the following content:

- many people are interested in holidaying in Antarctica
- specific attractions (scenery/wildlife?)
- available tours
- potential problems (distance/cold/environmental damage?)

Exercise 2

While listening to a passage, predict what the speaker(s) might say next.

 EXAMPLE:

What do you think the following speaker is going to talk about next?

'At school we learned how to read and write English but we never did much practice in listening or speaking. So when I went to my first lecture in English ...'

The speaker might describe the way the lecturer spoke (accent/speed?) and talk about his comprehension difficulties (taking notes/understanding main points?).

What do you think the following speakers are going to say next?

'Joyce was standing at the top of a ladder painting the lounge ceiling when suddenly ...'

'I'd been waiting for the results of the test for three weeks and I was feeling more and more anxious. That morning I received ...'

'We took along the tent, a fridge, gas tanks, a portable shower, a motor-driven generator: We had everything—the only thing we forgot was to put petrol in the car About ten minutes after setting out ...'

'The most common means by which the AIDS virus spreads are ...'

'The most significant positive effect of the end of the Cold War has been the reduction in the possibility of an armed conflict in Europe. On the other hand, it also opens up the possibility of ...'

Sometimes you can predict very accurately what the speaker's next words will be.

 EXAMPLE:

'The advantages of the system are outweighed by the ...' (disadvantages)

'Last but ...' (not least)

Predict the next word or phrase in each of the following sentences.

1. *'In this case the means doesn't justify ...'*

2. *'We have to look at the problems of supply and ...'*

3. *'Antarctica, the great southern ...'*

4. *'Smoking and excessive weight significantly increase the chances of coronary ...'*

5. *'Nowadays typewriters are rapidly being replaced by ...'*

The more you expand your vocabulary by reading, the easier it is to make predictions.

Exercise 3

Listen to one of the Tape Exercises. Stop the tape in mid-sentence and try to predict what is going to be said next.

Exercises with a Study Partner

Exercise 1

Listen to a short passage once only, writing notes as you listen. When the passage ends, use your notes to tell your study partner as much as you can about the passage, recording your answers on tape. Listen to the original passage again to make sure you included all of the main points.

Exercise 2

Find (or draw) four pictures which have something in common: for example, four photographs of different people, four postcards with different scenes, four pictures of different cars. Give a set of four pictures to your study partner and describe one of the pictures. Ask your study partner to decide which picture you have described.

Exercise 3

Choose a taped listening passage. Write a series of questions based on the information in the passage and give your partner 30 seconds to read the questions before you play the tape once only. Listen to the tape together and discuss the answers.

Exercise 4

Write a series of statements based on the information in a recorded listening passage. Include some statements which are either false or for which there is no information in the passage. Give your partner 30 seconds to read the statements before you play the tape once only. Listen to the tape together and discuss the answers.

Exercise 5

Record a radio news item or short talk. Make a written summary of the main points and remove some information as in the Macquarie River Flooding example on page 110. Remember to include a separate column for answers.

Give the summary to your study partner. After 30 seconds play the tape once only. Your partner's task is to fill in the missing information while listening to the tape. Listen to the tape together and check the answers.

This exercise requires you to read, listen and write at the same time. As this difficult skill may be tested in the IELTS, you should do this exercise as often as possible before taking the test.

▶ **MATERIALS FOR FURTHER STUDY**

In developing your study program, you may find the following materials useful. Books with accompanying cassettes are indicated with an asterisk.

Ferguson, N. and M. O'Reilly. 1989. *English Telephone Conversations*. * Nelson.

Jones, L. 1984. *Ideas: Speaking and Listening Activities for Upper-Intermediate Students*. * Cambridge University Press.

Kirby, S. 1985. *Penguin Listening Skills*. * Penguin.

Lynch, T. 1983. *Study Listening: Understanding Lectures and Talks in English*. * Cambridge University Press.

McDowell, J. 1982. *Basic Listening*. * Edward Arnold.

Smith, P et al. 1986. *Studying in Australia: Listening Effectively*. * Nelson.

▶ UNIT 4 *Speaking*

'I studied English at school for ten years. I've been on holiday in Britain and I didn't have too many problems in making myself understood – I've even given a paper in English at an international congress. I just found I hadn't had enough practice in answering the kind of questions I was asked in IELTS.'

Moroccan IELTS candidate

▶ SPEAKING TEST DESCRIPTION

The Speaking Section of the IELTS Test consists of an interview which lasts between 11 and 15 minutes.

GENERAL TRAINING MODULE

Candidates for the General Training Module take the same speaking test as Academic Module candidates.

Before you begin the interview, you will be asked to fill out a one-page questionnaire called a curriculum vitae or 'c.v.'. The c.v. asks questions about your work experience, study experience, and personal interests. Your writing on the c.v. is not assessed as part of the test.

TASK 1

Fill in this sample c.v. This is similar to the c.v. you will be required to fill in before the interview.

FULL NAME ....

NATIONALITY ....

FIRST LANGUAGE ....

OTHER LANGUAGES ....

EDUCATIONAL QUALIFICATIONS ....

WORK EXPERIENCE ....

REASON FOR DOING IELTS TEST ....

FUTURE STUDY PLANS ....

HOBBIES OR INTERESTS ....

After completing the c.v., you will go into the interview room where you will meet an interviewer who is a native speaker of English. During the next 11–15 minutes, the interviewer will follow a standard pattern consisting of five stages.

Stage 1:   introductions and greetings; basic questions about the candidate

Stage 2:   questions about general topics

Stage 3:   the candidate asks the interviewer questions based on a task

Stage 4:   more detailed questions, particularly focusing on the candidate's future plans

Stage 5:   closing the interview.

▶ ## STRATEGIES FOR THE IELTS INTERVIEW

PREDICTING THE TOPICS

It is useful to predict what topics will occur in the interview. In order to do this, you should remember that all IELTS candidates around the world have the following in common:

1. they are generally over 18 years of age

2. they have already studied at high school

3. they may have some work experience

4. they have moved to or are planning to move to an English-speaking country

5. they may have a particular major field of study

6. they come from a place that the interviewer probably has not been to or does not know well

7. they are planning to enter tertiary or further education

8. they are not native-speakers of English.

TASK 2*

Think of appropriate questions for these eight points above. The first one has been done as an example.

1. they are generally over 18 years of age.

    Are you married?

    Do you have any children?

    Do you live with your family?

TASK 3

Look at the sample c.v. below. You are now in the same situation as the interviewer: you have never met this person before. What questions would you ask this candidate?

FULL NAME ...*Antonella Marchini*...

NATIONALITY ...*Italian*...

FIRST LANGUAGE ...*Italian*..

OTHER LANGUAGES ...*English, German*...

EDUCATIONAL QUALIFICATIONS ...*High School Diploma*............................

WORK EXPERIENCE ...—..

REASON FOR DOING IELTS TEST ...*To study at University*.......................

FUTURE STUDY PLANS ...*Bachelor of Economics*...................................

HOBBIES OR INTERESTS ...*Music and tennis*.......................................

TASK 4

Look at your own c.v. form. What questions do you think an interviewer could ask you?

TASK 5

Study the following situations. What questions would you ask the person in each situation?

A foreigner has just arrived in your country.

An acquaintance tells you that she is planning to study physics at university.

You meet a person who works at IBM.

A relative is going to study in the United States.

A friend tells you he is writing an essay for university.

A friend has returned from a trip to the UK.

To summarise: although it is not possible to predict precisely what topics will be covered in an IELTS interview, it is reasonable to assume that the interviewer will focus on the candidate's past experience in work or study, way of life, views on the world, personal experiences, plans for future study, and feelings about moving to another country.

UNDERSTANDING THE QUESTIONS

The IELTS interview is not a test of listening comprehension; that is the aim of the Listening Section. The interviewer will generally speak quite clearly and try to make sure that you understand. The interviewer's goal is to hear you speak. You need, nevertheless, to understand the interviewer's questions so that you can respond appropriately. Remember that the same question can be asked in different ways.

TASK 6*

Match the questions in the left-hand column with those that have the same meaning in the right-hand column. Note that questions in the left- hand column may correspond to more than one question in the right- hand column. The first is done for you as an example.

1. What's your opinion of ... ?	A. How different is . . . ?
2. Do you feel that ... ?	B. How is it that ... ?
3. How do you find ... ?	C. How do you feel about ... ?
4. What's the difference between ... ?	D. Is (X) similar to ... ?
5. How come ... ?	E. Why... ?
6. How often ... ?	F. What do you think of ... ?
7. In what way ... ?	G. How...?
8. Where ... ?	H. How frequently ... ?
9. How far ... ?	I. Whereabouts ... ?
	J. To what extent ... ?
	K. What's your feeling on ... ?
	L. Do you think that ... ?

☞ EXAMPLE:

Direct questions:
'What are you going to study?'

Indirect questions:
'Could you tell me what you are going to study?'
'Do you know what you're going to study?'

Confirming questions:
'You're going to study Economics, are you?'
'You're going to study Economics, aren't you?'
'You're going to study Economics?'

Requests/instructions:
'Would you like to tell me a bit about your study plans?'
'Tell me what you're going to study.'

TASK 7

Ask the following questions in as many ways as possible.

1. Where were you born?

2. What part of the city do you live in?

3. What are the main tourist attractions in your country?

4. Where have you studied English?

5. How many brothers and sisters have you got?

6. What's the climate like in your country?

7. What are typical working hours in your country?

8. What aspect of English do you find most difficult?

9. Have you been collecting stamps for a long time?

10. What is the biggest social problem in your country?

ASKING FOR CLARIFICATION

In contrast to the Listening section, you have more control in the Interview. If you do not understand the interviewer's questions, you can use the following strategies.

If, for example, the interviewer says: *'Do you like travelling on the Tube?'* You can say that you don't understand: *'I'm sorry. I don't understand.'* *'Sorry. I don't follow.'*

You can ask for a question to be repeated: *'I didn't catch that. Would you mind repeating it?'* *'Could you repeat the question, please?'*

You can clarify the meaning of specific words or phrases you don't understand: *'Sorry. I don't know what you mean by 'Tube'.' 'Would you mind explaining 'Tube'?'*

You can check your understanding of a question: *'Do you mean the underground trains?' 'You're asking me about underground trains are you?' 'You're asking me if I like travelling on the Tube?'*

TASK 8

How would you respond if an interviewer asked you the following questions?

1. What's your opinion of topiary?

2. Could you tell me about the nard industry in your country?

3. Is myrosin commonly used in fermentation?

RESPONDING APPROPRIATELY

Each stage of the interview focuses on specific speaking skills. You need to respond appropriately to the interviewer's questions and instructions in each stage.

Stage 1 (1–2 minutes)

In this first stage, the interviewer:

- greets you

- invites you to sit down

- asks you for your c.v. form

- checks your identity

- turns on a cassette recorder (a recording may be made of interviews so that the examiners can check the interview procedure)

- asks you some questions from the c.v. form

Try to imagine the first minute of your interview. How will the interviewer greet you? How can you respond?

TASK 9

Ask a study partner to fill out a c.v. Your partner plays the role of interviewee and you play the role of interviewer. Role-play each part of Stage 1, beginning with the interviewee coming into the room. Greet your partner and ask him/her as many questions as possible. After completing the task, swap roles.

First impressions are very important. In all interviews—for jobs, college or university entrance—a confident candidate has a better chance of impressing the interviewer than a nervous and uncertain candidate.

Stage 2 (3–4 minutes)

The interviewer does not tell you that Stage 2 has begun. You do not need to recognise the move from Stage 1 to 2.

In Stage 2, the interviewer gives you an opportunity to speak for longer periods, giving more detailed information and opinions.

Topics from Stage 1 may be used to do this. You might also be asked to describe how something is done, how something works or what something is like. If you are taking the IELTS test in an English-speaking country, you may be asked to compare aspects of life in that country with life in your country of origin.

   EXAMPLE:

'Could you tell me what happens at a wedding in your country?'

'How do you make X (a well-known food in your country)?'

'How do people in your country learn English?'

'Tell me what the procedure is for obtaining a driving licence in your country. '

'So, you really like hockey. Can you describe the rules?'

'In what ways is English used in your country?'

'How different is your life from the lives of your parents/grandparents?'

'How does the cost of living here (an English-speaking country) compare with your country?'

TASK 10*

In Stage 1, a candidate says that although he now lives in Brasilia, he originally comes from Rio de Janeiro. What Stage 2 questions can you make from this information?

TASK 11

Look at your own c.v. and decide what Stage 2 questions you might be asked by the interviewer.

GIVING AN ORGANISED ANSWER

You need to organise detailed answers so that they are clear to the listener.

Before beginning to answer the question, it is possible to comment on it by saying, for example, 'That's a difficult question'/'That's a very interesting question'. If you use this strategy, it will give you a little more time to prepare an organised answer.

In organising your answer, it may be useful (as in writing) to begin with a sentence or phrase that gives a summary of the main points you are going to talk about. This will help your listener to follow your answer.

 EXAMPLE:

Interviewer: 'Why do you want to study X?'

Candidate: 'That's a rather difficult question. There are two main reasons, I suppose.'

The summary phrase is: 'There are two main reasons, I suppose.' This provides a structure for the rest of the answer, which describes each of the reasons.

TASK 12

What summary sentences or phrases would you use in your answers to the following questions?

1. What did you study at high school?

2. Which is the most popular sport in your country?

3. How do people spend their weekends in your home town?

4. Could you tell me why you chose to study at the University of X?

The summary sentence you choose provides the structure for your main points.

 EXAMPLE:

Interviewer: 'What is the procedure for getting a driving licence in your country?'

Candidate: 'Oh, it's fairly simple: there are only a few things you have to do. First ... Then ... After that ... And then finally ... '

TASK 13

Listen to Tape Exercise 7. Sandy's answer to the question 'What was the course like?' gives an example of a well-organised answer. Note Sandy's summary sentence and her organisation of the two main points.

TASK 14

Continue the candidate's answers to the following questions. Record and analyse your answers, paying particular attention to their organisation.

Interviewer: *'Why do you want to study X?'* (your subject)
Candidate: *'Well, for many reasons. Firstly, I ...'*

Interviewer: *'Tell me a bit about your educational background.'*
Candidate: *'Well, first I went to ...'*

Interviewer: *'Do you find American English easier to understand than British English?'*
Candidate: *'Yes, I do/No, I don't ...'*

Interviewer: *'I've never been to your country. What's it like?'*
Candidate: *'That's a big question ...'*

Interviewer: *'Which is the best university in your country?'*
Candidate: *'I suppose X is, because ...'*

TASK 15

Record and analyse your answers to the following questions, paying particular attention to their organisation.

1. What sports are played in your country?
2. Could you describe the traditional architecture of your country?
3. What role does religion have in everyday life in your country?
4. What would you regard as the most significant events in your country's recent history?
5. How aware do you think people are nowadays about environmental issues?

You also need to show the interviewer that you have said everything you want to say. There are several ways to do this.

You can repeat the summary sentence, perhaps changing it slightly: 'Yes, as I was saying, *it's very difficult to generalise'* 'Yes, there really are many reasons.'

You can state that you have finished: *'I think that's all ' 'I can't think of anything else ' 'That's it, I think '*

You can check the interviewer's understanding: *'Have I answered your question?' 'Does that give you a clear idea? '*

TASK 16

Answer the following questions, paying particular attention to the way you conclude your answers.

1. What are sporting facilities like in your home town?

2. What role does tourism play in your country's economy?

3. How serious is unemployment in your country?

4. Can you describe one of the main festivals celebrated in your country?

5. In your opinion what are the most serious problems associated with modern city life?

Stage 3 (3-4 minutes)

So far you have been answering the interviewer's questions. Now, in Stage 3, the interviewer wants to hear you ask questions. In order to give you an opportunity to ask questions, he or she describes a situation in which you must find out some information.

The tasks will usually be about service/social survival situations and study-related situations in an English-speaking country. Generally, your role is to ask for information or assistance which helps you to solve a 'problem'.

Example 1

The interviewer says:

> *'I work in an airline office. You want to book a flight to Bogota next month. Please read this and ask me questions '*

You are handed a sheet of paper similar to the one below which gives you the information which you must use to form questions.

FLIGHT INFORMATION

You want to book a flight to Bogota. Imagine that the interviewer works in a travel agency. Ask the interviewer questions about the flight.

Find out about:

a. frequency of flights

b. departure times

c. duration of flight

d. number of stop-overs

e. price of ticket.

Example 2

The interviewer says:

> 'Now, I'd like to hear you ask me questions. I've just received this gift in the post. Ask me as many different questions in as many different ways as you can. This sheet explains what to do and it suggests the questions you should ask.'

She then starts unwrapping a gift and hands you the following sheet.

A GIFT

The interviewer has just received a gift. Ask him or her as much as you can about the gift.

Find out about:

a. sender of the gift

b. interviewer's relationship with the sender

c. reason for the gift

d. type of gift

e. interviewer's reactions to the gift

Example 3

The interviewer says:

> '...Thanks very much. That was really interesting. Now, at this stage, I want you to ask me some questions. Please ask me as many questions as possible. Here is the situation: You've never played tennis before and you're really interested in learning. So you decide to take a course of tennis lessons. You're really busy at the moment, so you go to the tennis school to find a course which fits into your schedule.'

He hands you the following sheet:

TENNIS LESSONS

You have never played tennis before and you want to enrol in a course of tennis lessons. Find out which course fits into your schedule.

Find out about:

a. levels of courses available

b. duration of courses

c. cost of courses

d. times of courses

e. size of class

---

continued on page 131

EXAMPLE 3 – TENNIS LESSONS: *continued from page 130*

Your Schedule:				
SATURDAY:	9.00–12.00	Swimming class	1.00–6.00	Library study
SUNDAY:	9.00–12.00	Swimming classes	1.00–6.00	Horseriding
MONDAY:	8.00– 4.00	University		
TUESDAY:	8.00–12.00	University	5.00–9.00	French class
WEDNESDAY:	2.00– 4.00	University		
THURSDAY:	1.00– 3.00	Chess club		
FRIDAY:	10.00–11.00	University	1.00–6.00	Library study

Read the information sheet before you begin. If you do not understand the task or any of the words on the sheet, ask the interviewer to explain before you begin.

ASKING QUESTIONS CORRECTLY

You must ask a question about every point which the sheet instructs you to 'find out about'. When you have done this, you may then add some more questions of your own about the topic. Your questions should be relevant to the task and correctly formed. You need to develop your confidence in forming correct questions.

TASK 17*

Make questions from the following phrases which are taken from Example 1 on page 129. The first one has been done for you.

1. Frequency of flights: *How often do flights leave for Bogota?* ....

2. Departure times: ....

3. Duration of flight: ....

4. Number of stop-overs: ....

5. Price of ticket: ....

TASK 18*

The interviewer says: *'I am a real estate agent. You want to rent an apartment. We are looking at an apartment together: Read this and ask me questions.'*

> ### RENTING AN APARTMENT
> #### Find out about:
>
> 1. Garage?   *Is there a garage in the apartment building* ....?
> 2. A television?   ....?
> 3. Schools near here? ....?
> 4. Air-conditioning? ....?
> 5. Deposit?   ....?

Make questions from the phrases on the sheet. The first one has been done for you.

TASK 19

Refer to the list of social and study situations on page 99 of this book. Write or record on cassette as many questions as you can which are appropriate in these situations. Work with a study partner or take all the roles in the situation yourself. Ask a teacher or another native speaker of English to check if your questions are correct.

TASK 20

Choose advertisements from English-language newspapers and magazines. Ask as many questions as you can about the advertised product or service.

 EXAMPLE:

> ### Learn English in England
> The Royal English College in Manchester provides intensive summer courses at all levels. The college, situated near the city centre, can also provide home-stay accommodation if required. For more information please write to P.O. Box 99, Manchester, UK.

continued on page 137

Task 20 *continued from page 137*

Sample Questions:

1. How many hours per week do students study in the intensive courses?
2. How long do the courses last?
3. How much does the course cost?
4. Where is Manchester?
5. How many students are there in each class?
6. Does the College organise any excursions?

TASK 21

Choose any passage in English and transform the statements into questions.

☞ EXAMPLE: (from a newspaper article):

BOOST FOR RURAL SPORT

The Minister for Sport and Recreation, Mr. John Bottomly, announced yesterday that the government would provide five million dollars to fund a building program of sports centres in rural centres throughout the eastern part of the state of Victoria. The Minister went on to say that people living in country areas had been seriously disadvantaged in the past and this program would provide more equality.

Sample Questions:

1. Who is Mr John Bottomly?
2. Who is the Minister for Sport?
3. What did the Minister for Sport announce yesterday?
4. How much money will the government provide?
5. What will the money be used for?
6. Where will the sports centres be built?
7. Which part of the state will the centres be built in?
8. Why has the government decided to fund the building program?

TASK 22

How many questions can you ask in 60 seconds? Record yourself doing Task 21 on cassette and then check how many questions you asked and how many mistakes you made. Do this exercise every day and make a chart or graph to track your progress.

PLAYING A ROLE

In the situations in Stage 3, both you and the interviewer are, in a sense, playing roles.

To play your role well, you have to understand

- who your character is
- what your character needs
- what relationship your character has with the character played by the interviewer.

The language you use should reflect these three points.

 EXAMPLE:

The interviewer says:

'You have just arrived in Edinburgh for the first time. You go to a Tourist Information Centre. I am working at the information desk in the Centre. Ask me as many questions as possible. Read this first. It will help you to form questions.'

A VISIT TO EDINBURGH
Find out about:

a. hotel accommodation

b. price of accommodation

c. distance from the city centre

d. city sights

e. entertainment facilities

f. transport

Who is your character?

You might decide that your character is a tourist, a business person, or an overseas student.

You can make the situation more realistic by giving some information about your character. For example, if you decide you are a tourist, you could say: 'I've just arrived from the airport and this is my first time in this city ... '

You should begin the role play appropriately. If you were entering a Tourist Information Centre, you would greet the clerk. For example: 'Good morning. Could you help me?'

What does your character need?

You need to get all of the information required on the information sheet. When you have finished, there may be an opportunity for you to ask additional questions.

You must follow the character's needs. In reality, you may, for example, know Edinburgh very well. The character you play does not, so you need to get all of the information required. In reality, you may also want to ask about different aspects of Edinburgh not listed on the sheet. In your character, however, you must ask the required questions first before attempting to ask any other questions.

***What relationship does your character have with the character played
by the interviewer?***

As in most service encounters, you are strangers. As a result, your language needs to
reflect this. For example: 'Could you tell me something about the city sights. I'll be in
Edinburgh for just three days.' would be more appropriate than 'I want to know about
the city sights'.

When the interviewer answers your questions, you must listen and respond appropriately. The interviewer's answer influences your response.

  EXAMPLE:

Candidate (playing the role of an enquirer at a tennis school):
'How many different levels do you have in your tennis courses?'

Interviewer (playing the role of a tennis school receptionist):
'Well, we've got a level for everybody, sir. Beginners, Intermediate, and Advanced.'

Candidate:
*'That's good. I'm interested in the Beginners' course. Could you tell me when the
courses are held?'*

TASK 23

Role-play the following Stage 3 tasks. You should cover all of the points on
each information sheet in no more than four minutes. Record and analyse the
role-plays.

Situation 1:

The interviewer says:

> 'You are at the airport waiting for a bus to go to the city centre. You've been
> waiting for 20 minutes and the bus hasn't come. I'm also standing in the queue.
> Use this to ask me questions.'

TRANSPORT INFORMATION
Find out about:

a. frequency of buses

b. distance to city centre

c. other forms of transport available
(taxi, train, etc.)

d. cost of alternative transport

Situation 2:

The interviewer says:

'You have just arrived in New Zealand and you want to buy a second-hand car. I am the car salesman. You are interested in a small Toyota that we are both looking at. Before you ask me questions, please read this.'

BUYING A SECOND-HAND CAR
Find out about:

a. the price

b. the distance travelled

c. the age

d. possibility of discount

e. method of payment

Situation 3:

The interviewer says:

'I am a bank clerk. You are a customer and you want to open a bank account.'

OPENING A BANK ACCOUNT
Find out about:

a. types of account

d. credit cards

b. interest on accounts

e. bank charges

c. chequebooks

f. obtaining credit

Stage 4 (3–4 minutes)

In this stage, the interviewer continues the conversation, as in Stage 2. The interviewer speaks as little as possible in order to concentrate on what you are saying and make an assessment of your language proficiency. The questions you are asked in this section will emerge naturally from the conversation and may be drawn from your curriculum vitae.

As in Stage 2, you need to organise your answers by having a summary sentence, a clearly marked structure and an appropriate closing strategy.

In Stage 4 the interviewer asks you to express your opinion, give explanations, make detailed comparisons, or speculate about your future. You are required to speak for longer periods and in more detail. In the following examples, the candidates respond very successfully to the interviewer's probing questions.

Example 1

The candidate works in a chemical laboratory:

Interviewer: 'If you were the head of your institution what changes would you introduce?'

Candidate: 'I'd love to be in that situation. The first thing I'd do is change the decision-making process. At the moment, decisions are made by the directorate and the workers have no chance to express their opinion. That would be the first thing I'd change '

Interviewer: 'But don't you think it would be more difficult to make decisions that way?'

Candidate: 'I don't know, but I'm sure they'd be better decisions '

Interviewer: 'Why do you say that?'

Candidate: 'Well, it obviously depends on the issue. If it involves conditions of work, then clearly the people working in the labs are the ones who understand that kind of issue best '

Interviewer: 'I'm not sure I agree with you. Don't you think that the directorate has a more objective view?'

Example 2

The candidate is an economist.

Interviewer: 'What made you decide to become an economist?'

Candidate: 'I've always been very interested in Economics.'

Interviewer: 'Could you elaborate on that?'

Candidate: 'Well, I don't think it's possible to understand, or to change, the way society works unless you've studied economics.'

Interviewer: 'What do you mean by "change society"?'

Candidate: 'I suppose what I mean is ... '

TASK 24

Using your c.v., role-play Stage 4 with your study partner. The 'interviewer' should press the 'candidate' for as much information as possible, using the following question types:

Questions which seek elaboration:
'Could you tell me more about X?'
'Could you elaborate on X?'
'What do you mean precisely by X?'

Questions which seek explanation:
'Could you explain why X?'
'How is X possible?'

Questions which seek justification:
'I don't agree. Don't you think that X?'
'Why do you say that?'

In giving detailed answers, you may need time to pause and reflect before you continue. In order to gain time to think you can use 'fillers' such as:
let me see; let's see; well; how can I put it?; I'm not sure; I mean; you know; I'll have to think about it.

FINDING THE RIGHT WORDS

> *'I knew exactly what I wanted to say, but there were two or three important words I didn't know in English. I just froze.'*
>
> Norwegian IELTS candidate

If you find yourself in this situation, you should explain what you mean by using other words. This strategy will be regarded positively by the interviewer.

  EXAMPLES:

The interviewer asks you: *'What do you think have been the most important changes in your field over the past five years?'*

You are an agronomist and you would like to say: *'Mechanisation has been the most significant change '*

You do not know or cannot recall the word *'mechanisation'* in English. You can say: *'Five years ago young trees were planted by hand and this was a very slow process. Today we have machines that plant young trees. They can easily plant a thousand trees a day. That has been the biggest change during the past five years.'*

You are an urban planner and you would like to say: 'Environmental impact awareness'.

You do not know or cannot recall this term in English. You can say: '*Nowadays ordinary people care more about the quality of life in cities – for example, they worry about air pollution, rubbish, and clean water We have to study the effects which our plans have on these things. That's the greatest change*'.

TASK 25

Think of terms associated with your field which you do not know in English. Explain these terms using other words and phrases.

TASK 26

Answer the following questions. Record and analyse your answers.

What are you going to major in?
In your answer, speak about:

subjects   employment possibilities.
your reasons

Are you going to do your own cooking when you are at university?
In your answer, speak about:

intentions   preferences
experience   potential difficulties.

Have you decided where you're going to live while you're studying?
In your answer, speak about:

intentions   uncertainties.
preferences

Some local students feel that overseas students get preferential treatment. What is your opinion?
In your answer, give:

your opinion   a justification.

Do you think you'll be able to cope with the English-language demands of your intended study program?
In your answer:

predict language demands/give examples
assess your language skills/give examples
predict your performance.

TASK 27

In this task, your aim is to speak spontaneously and fluently about a range of subjects. Your study partner chooses topics of interest taken from the newspaper, television or radio. For example:

'Twenty people were killed in a bus accident yesterday.'

Your study partner then interviews you about the topic. For example:

- What do you think the main causes of road accidents are?
- How do you think road accidents can be prevented?
- Do you think the government is doing enough to improve road safety?

Try to speak for at least a minute on each subject, using 'fillers' if necessary. If you pause for more than three seconds without using an appropriate filler, you must stop. You then ask your partner a question to see if he or she can speak for a minute without stopping.

TASK 28

Answer the following questions. Record, transcribe, and analyse your answers.

1. If you hadn't studied X, what field would you have chosen?
2. What qualities does a good teacher need?
3. What do you see yourself doing in five years' time?
4. What is successful communication, in your opinion?
5. What are your goals in life?

Stage 5 (1 minute)

In this final stage, the interviewer will conclude the interview. He/she may:

- say that it was very nice to meet you
- wish you good luck
- say that he/she hopes to meet you again
- say goodbye.

How would you respond?

You have now finished a 15-minute interview. You leave the room and the interviewer decides on a score for you. How is this assessed? What has the interviewer been looking for?

'Many candidates seem to be really worried about getting their grammar right in the interview, which is a pity, because often they communicate quite well.

IELTS interviewer

When the IELTS interviewer assesses your speaking, she or he may do it differently from the way you assess your own speaking. The key question in the interviewer's assessment will be: How successful was the candidate's communication? In order to make this assessment, the interviewer must answer a number of questions:

Q: Did the candidate's pronunciation disturb the communication? Could I understand the candidate easily?

This is not the same as the question: 'Was the candidate's pronunciation correct?'. Almost everybody who learns a foreign language as an adult has pronunciation which in some way is different from the pronunciation of native speakers of that language.

There are three main aspects of your pronunciation which may create difficulties in communication. These involve the differences between your native language and English in consonants, in vowels, and in stress and intonation. Where the differences are greatest, communication may be difficult.

TASK 29

Record a native speaker of English from radio or television. The recording should be about 1 minute long. Make a transcript of the recording and read the transcript aloud, recording yourself as you do this.

Compare your version with the original, assessing the differences. Use whatever resources you have access to: study partner, native speaker, or teacher. Decide where the greatest differences are and practise those parts of the transcript. Read the transcript again, record and reassess yourself.

Q: Did the candidate's grammar disturb the communication? Was the meaning clear? Were only short simple sentences used? Were the questions correctly formed?

TASK 30

Record yourself speaking for about two minutes, perhaps choosing one of the tasks in this unit. Do not prepare what you are going to say. Do not write notes before you speak. Listen to your recording and write out an exact transcript.

Check for grammatical mistakes. If possible ask a teacher or a study partner to check the transcript. Make a list of any mistakes you have made and focus on these grammatical areas in your program of reading, listening, writing, and grammar development.

☞ EXAMPLES: (an extract from a student's transcript)

I wanted to study in America – I think it has very good universities – but my father suggested me to go to Germany.

The student then checked for errors and found the following:

'*my father suggested me to go*'

SHOULD BE

'*my father suggested that I go/should go*'

In his study program, the student used two strategies:

- While carrying out listening tasks, he began listening for examples of the use of 'suggest'.
- He drilled himself in the correct form by repeating '*My father suggested that I should go to Germany*', and other versions of this structure, for example '*My mother suggested that I should study in Belgium*', and '*My brother suggested that I should stay here*' He did this until he could use the structure without hesitation.

Q: Does the candidate communicate effectively?

Think of any two people you know who are native speakers of your first language. Ask yourself which person is the better communicator? Although both probably have very similar grammar, pronunciation, and vocabulary, it should be possible to decide that one is better.

The following checklist presents some of the key characteristics of effective communication:

SPEAKER'S PURPOSE
- very clear
- fairly clear
- unclear

ORGANISATION OF MAIN POINT
- very clear
- fairly clear
- unclear

VOLUME
- too loud
- just right
- not loud enough

SPEED
- too fast
- just right
- too slow

EYE CONTACT[1]
- maintains eye contact
- avoids eye contact

FEEDBACK[2]
- always
- sometimes
- never

BODY LANGUAGE[3]
- appears nervous
- appears relaxed

CONTENT
- totally relevant
- sometimes irrelevant
- totally irrelevant

1. Generally speaking, your interviewer will respond positively if you maintain eye contact most of the time while speaking and listening.

2. Good listeners show interest and understanding by providing feedback. There are many forms of feedback, including: nodding the head, saying 'mm' (particularly common in English), saying 'I see', 'right', etc. (when appropriate).

   Good speakers check to see whether their listeners understand and are showing interest by checking for feedback. If they do not receive feedback, they may ask questions such as 'Do you understand what I mean?' or say 'You look puzzled'.

3. All candidates are nervous. This is sometimes expressed physically with fidgeting and awkward posture, for example, which can disturb the communication. Good candidates know what to expect in the interview (topics, tasks, and requirements), and therefore try to appear relaxed and in control.

TASK 31

Ask a study partner to interview you in English. During the interview your study partner should assess your behaviour using the checklist above. After the interview, discuss the results of the checklist with your partner. If you have access to video equipment, you can record the interview and analyse your own presentation.

▶ **TEST-TAKING STRATEGIES**

> '*I got so nervous in the interview that I couldn't even open my mouth.*'
> Russian IELTS candidate

PREPARING FOR THE INTERVIEW

Make sure you have role-played the whole interview as many times as you can.

Maintain a constant dialogue with yourself in English. If you are not in a situation where you can speak aloud, do the exercises mentally. The more you practise in this way, the easier it will be for you to 'think in English' and respond more easily during the interview.

On small cards which you can carry round with you, make a list of the questions suggested in this unit. Shuffle the cards, take one out of the pack and then give an answer. Keep inventing new questions for your pack. You can practise these whenever you have spare time. If you are with other people, on public transport for example, you can still give your answers in your head. Note, however, that the Interview assesses your ability to speak spontaneously. If the interviewer feels that you are giving a rehearsed answer, he or she may shift the topic immediately.

ON THE DAY OF THE INTERVIEW

Make sure you arrive at the interview having practised the same day. Role-play the whole procedure up to the moment you enter the interview room. Although the examiner will help you to 'warm-up' in Stage 1, it is useful if you can 'warm yourself up' by speaking in English before going into the room.

▶ MATERIALS FOR FURTHER STUDY

Asterisked materials are accompanied by cassettes.

Baker. A. 1977. *Ship or Sheep? An Intermediate Pronunciation Course.** Cambridge University Press.

Bradford, B. 1985. *Intonation in Context: Intonation Practice for Upper-Intermediate and Advanced Learners of English* * Cambridge University Press.

Hadfield, J. 1987. *Advanced Communication Games: a Collection of Games and Activities for Intermediate and Advanced Students of English.* Nelson.

Jones, L. 1984. *Ideas: Speaking and Listening Activities for Upper-Intermediate Students.** Cambridge University Press.

Kench, A.B. 1980. *Asking Questions: Notes, Exercises and Dialogues on How to Ask Questions in English.* Macmillan.

Ladousse, G.P. 1983. *Speaking Personally: Quizzes and Questionnaires for Fluency Practice.* Cambridge University Press.

Morgan, J. and M. Rinvolucri. 1988. *The Q Book: Practising Interrogatives in Reading, Speaking And Writing.* Longman.

Mortimer, C. 1985. *Elements of Pronunciation: Intensive Practice for Intermediate and More Advanced Students.* * Cambridge University Press.

Pifer, G. and N. Mutoh. 1988. *Point Counterpoint: Discussion and Persuasion Techniques.* Newbury House.

Rudska, B. et al. 1981. *The Words You Need.* Macmillan.

Watcynlones, P. 1978. *Act English: A Book of Role Plays* Penguin.

UNIT 3: LISTENING

Speaker: Tape Exercise 1 (see Sample Task 1, page 102). Liz is phoning Michael. She wants to arrange to meet him tonight. Decide which of the pictures best fits what you hear on the tape, and circle the letter under that picture. We have done the first one for you as an example. As you listen to the tape, circle the correct answer. First read questions 1 to 3.

Now answer questions 1 to 3.

Liz: Hi, Michael. How are things?

Michael: Hi, Liz. Good, thanks. What's new with you?

Liz: Oh, I was just wondering if you wanted to go out tonight.

Michael: Well ... I was thinking of going to the University Library to do a bit of study. What've you got in mind?

Liz: I thought we could just go for a walk. Maybe down to that park near the beach.

Michael: Tonight?! You must be joking – it's too cold. What about coming round to my place? We could just watch TV or something.

Liz: Watch TV?! That's all you ever want to do! I want to go out somewhere. That new Jane Fonda film is on in town. How about that?

Michael: Look, if you really want to go somewhere, you could come with me to the library.

Liz: Oh, come on.

Michael: OK. Just joking. What time does it start?

Liz: Oh, I think it's half past eight or something. I'll just get the paper and have a look. Just hang on for a minute.

Liz: Don't be silly. You'll love it. It got a fantastic review in the paper last week.

Michael: OK. OK. So, where are we going to meet?

Liz: It'd be easiest if we met at the cinema.

Michael: OK. Where is it?

Liz: Oh, you know. The Odeon.

Michael: Where is that?

Liz: Well, you know where the Town Hall is?

Michael: Yeah.

Liz: Well. Walk up Market Street past the Co-op Bookshop and turn left into Pitt Street. Then you go along Pitt Street as far as the park on the corner and you'll see it. It's right in front of the park.

Michael: Oh, yeah. I know where it is. OK. Look, I'll meet you there at quarter past eight.

Liz: What about you? Are you going to take the car?

Michael: I'd love to, but the battery's flat.

Liz: So what are you going to do?

Michael: Well, I can't catch a train or a bus. They're still on strike.

Liz: Oh, yeah. I forgot about that.

Michael: I could get a taxi, I suppose.

Liz: Get a taxi? How long is it since you caught a taxi? It'll cost you a fortune.

Michael: Yeah, I suppose you're right. It's not that far – it's only three stops on the bus after all. Won't take me long to walk.

Liz: I thought you said it was too cold to walk.

Speaker: Tape Exercise 2 (see Sample Task 2, page 104). Gerharde has just moved to a new area of town and wants to join the local library. A librarian is filling in an application form, asking Gerharde for details. Look at questions 4 to 7. Now answer questions 4 to 7.

Librarian: Yes, and we're open on Saturdays too, but only until 4.00 o'clock. OK. Now, I just have to take a few details down from you and then we're right.

Gerharde: All right. Fine.

Librarian: Could I have your full name, please?

Gerharde: It's Gerharde Esterhazy.

Librarian: Now, hang on. Is Gerharde your first name?

Gerharde: Yes.

Librarian: So, that's – let me see – G-A-

Gerharde: No. It's G-E-R-H-A-R-D-E.

Librarian: -H-A-R-D-E .

Gerharde: Esterhazy. E-S-T-E-R-H-A-Z-Y.

Librarian: H-A-Z-Y. Mm, I don't think I've heard that name before. Now, can I have your date of birth Miss Esterhazy, please?

Gerharde: Sure. December the seventh, 1955.

Librarian: Hmm. Seven, twelve, fifty-five – a Sagittarian like me. And where do you live, Miss Esterhazy?

Gerharde: 13 Albion Street. A-L-B-I-O-N. Leichhardt. 2040.

Librarian: Right. Oh, that's a lovely street. Now, last question. Your phone number, please.

Gerharde: You mean at home?

Librarian: Or in the office, if you prefer.

Gerharde: OK. My office number is 567 4990.

Librarian: OK. Fine. You can pick your card up tomorrow, and then you can start borrowing immediately.

Speaker: Tape Exercise 3 (see Task 7, page 106). Part 1. Write down the numbers you hear.

890

15,640

33

234,980

1,435,756

742

387,313

569,030

781,953

54,278

63,726,867

99.21563

84.034

⅝

⁹⁄₁₀

23.3

34.3

89.074

12 ½

99.9

Speaker: Part 2. Write down the prices you hear.

$1500

£99.90

$2500

$13.33

$30.13

£27.14

Speaker: Part 3. Write down the dates you hear.

1965

April 20

1982

May 15

1799

August 2 1

1804

1939

September 8

1968

Speaker: Part 4. Write down the telephone numbers you hear.

889 9745

919 5392

465 6578
02 891 653
987 344
608 6662
008 750 11 65

Speaker: Tape Exercise 4 (see Task 8, page 106). Write down the following groups of letters.

AAI
QKY
WUTT
HJP
JGE
BYI
AEH
RVG
EEB
IIE
BVD
PBD
SCE
RKO
IVT

Speaker: Tape Exercise 5 (see Task 9, page 106). Write down the following names.

1. Campbell
2. George
3. Christopher
4. Irene
5. Marco
6. Victoria
7. Hennessy
8. Winton
9. Cyril
10. Adelaide
11. Costello
12. Jerot
13. Glenda
14. Sitompul
15. Manchester
16. Ontario
17. Zoe
18. Leeds
19. Queensland
20. Harry.

Speaker: Tape Exercise 6 (see Sample Task 3, page 107). Jaedok attends an orientation talk given by the Overseas Students' Officer at his university. As you listen to the recording, answer questions 8-16 by circling T for 'True' and F for 'False'. The first one has been done for you as an example. First look at questions 8 to 16. You will hear the talk once only so write down the answers as you listen to the tape.

Betty June: Good morning, everybody. I'm Betty June, the Overseas Students' Officer, and on behalf of all of us here I'd like to welcome you to Dulacca Polytechnic. We very much hope that your stay here will be profitable and pleasant.

I'd like to begin by giving you some basic information on things that I know you'll be concerned about. Now, of course the most urgent matter is your enrolment. You've already been given written information about enrolment procedures. Could I just emphasise the deadline: you must enrol by January 25th at the latest. It's very important that you do this for legal reasons – you can't remain in this country after that date on a student visa unless you're enrolled If there are any more questions about enrolment, please don't hesitate to speak with Ms Fluerty after morning tea. Once you've enrolled, there are a number of other bureaucratic things which you should do so you'll be free to concentrate on your studies when courses begin on March 6.

The first thing to do when you've enrolled is to pick up your identity cards. Most of you here are doing postgrad courses and so you should get your ID cards from the Postgraduate Student Office. That's all of you apart from the people doing the BA courses—you should go to the Undergraduate Studies Office. That's the red-brick building opposite the Students' Union. Once you've got your ID, you need to pick up another card at the library. You should go to the enquiries counter on the ground floor of the library. If you present your student identity card they'll make up a library borrowing card and you'll be able to borrow books immediately and of course use all the other facilities. It probably sounds a bit complicated but it's really very simple. If you've got any questions about this or anything else don't forget that we're here to help. During term, the Overseas Student Office is open from 9 to 6.30 but in the enrolment period just from 10 to 5.

The next thing you're probably thinking about is money. Ms Holly from the National Bank here on campus will be speaking to you this afternoon and she'll answer any specific questions about banking procedures, transferring money and so on. I'll just say that the bank here is open from 9 to 4 Monday to Fridays. That should serve all your banking needs. If you do find yourself in any kind of difficulty you should of course come and speak to us and we'll try to sort things out. We don't normally cash cheques at the Overseas Student Office but in an emergency we do.

The last practical thing you need to know is how to get medical assistance. The Polytechnic has its own health centre. The service is free of charge for all enrolled students and I think you'll find Dr Gisler very helpful and efficient. You can make an appointment with her by ringing extension 870—that's 870—or by going directly to the centre. The doctor sees patients all day Monday to Friday and on Saturday mornings. We hope you won't have to see the doctor but if you do you know you're in good hands. Now let's see what else? Oh yes. Sports facilities. As you've probably already seen on your tour of the campus we have an excellent gymnasium with its own indoor pool, open seven days a week from 9 in the morning to 9 at night. There's no charge for the use of facilities in the gym for students enrolled at Dulacca but you must show your student ID card. The tennis courts are also available seven days a week but you must book with Mr Lucas on extension 638. Again, use of the courts is free of charge to all enrolled students ...

Speaker: Tape Exercise 7 (see Sample Task 4, page 108). Richard is interviewing an applicant for a job in the office where he works. He is asking the applicant about her experience at university. Listen to their conversation and answer Questions 17 to 25 by writing a word or a short phrase in the space provided. Now look at Questions 17 to 25.

Now answer questions 17 to 25.

Richard: Well, I see from your c.v., Sandy, that you studied at University College. How did you find it there?

Sandy: I had a great time. The teaching was good and I made a lot of great friends. The psychology department was a great place to be.

Richard: So how come you chose psychology?

Sandy: Well at first I didn't have any clear idea of what I wanted to do after university— I didn't say to myself 'I want to be a clinical psychologist or a researcher or anything like that'. I suppose I've just always been interested in people and the way they act. I wanted to know why people think and act the way they do. It's a fascinating area.

Richard: And what was the course like?

Sandy: Like I said, it was just great. The teachers were all really friendly and they had this special approach to teaching. You know, they didn't just give us lectures and tell us to read books like they might do in some more traditional places. The whole course was based on a problem-solving approach—you know, they'd describe a particular situation to us and we'd speculate about what might happen. And after that we'd do the reading and see if it confirmed our own ideas. That's what I liked best—the really practical orientation of the course. I learn very well with that style, so for me it was just great.

Richard: I see from your c.v. that you graduated in '86 and after that – let me see ...

Sandy: I got a job with the Department of Employment. It was only a temporary thing for about six months. I was a researcher in the department. I used to have to design questionnaires and things like that for surveys that they carried out. We'd design a survey, go out to the factories and ask all the questions to the workers and the management, and then go back to the office and analyse all the data. It was really very interesting. And I guess the psychology course at college helped me a lot. We did a whole unit on statistical analysis and that came in very useful for analysing the questionnaires and presenting the data in our reports. You know, I guess it really would have been very difficult if I hadn't had that kind of training.

Richard: And after that you worked for four years in an advertising agency. That must have been a bit of a change from the Department of Employment, wasn't it?

Sandy: Well, not really. I guess the office furnishings were a bit more sophisticated but the job was fairly similar. I was basically still doing the same thing, designing question-naires, going out, asking questions and making reports. The only difference was that this time I wasn't asking people about their work. I was asking them what kind of wash-ing powder they'd bought and if they preferred Brand X to Brand Y. Then I'd make up a report and the agency would use the information in their advertising campaigns. I enjoyed it a lot.

Richard: So why did you leave?

Sandy: Well, four years is a long time to be asking people you know those sort of ques-tions about washing powder and shampoo ... no, seriously, after two years I was in charge of the research department of the agency and I had one assistant researcher. I guess after two years of doing that I suppose I felt, you know, I know I can do this well and now I want to do something else that's a little different. And there was nowhere for me to go inside the company. It just wasn't challenging for me any more and because I needed a challenge I decided to move on. When I heard about the position of Senior Researcher here at the institute I thought: that's exactly what I want—the chance to combine my management skills and my research interests working in a much larger department with more varied work.

Richard: And you felt that the job description in our advertisement would offer you the kind of challenge you are looking for?

Sandy: Exactly. Yes. As I said, management in a larger organisation and research com-bined. Also, to be honest with you, I heard about the job before it was advertised. A friend of mine who works here in the publications section—John Pincher?—told me a few weeks ago that you were looking for someone to take over the job. He described the position to me in quite a bit of detail and I thought well that's exactly what I'm looking for—so really I'd written my letter of application before the job was even advertised.

Richard: I should tell you that with the present cutbacks we've only got one full-time administrative assistant in the section. How would you feel about doing your own word processing, typing, that sort of thing?

Sandy: Oh I'm used to that—I've done all my own word processing for ages. It's the only way to write really, isn't it? I can type well—about sixty words a minute. I did a secretar-ial course after I left school so I learned typing and shorthand and then a few years later I bought a p.c. and I taught myself how to do word processing too.

Richard: Well that's handy. Now, in the position you've applied for you'd have five assis-tant researchers responsible to you. That's considerably more responsibility than you've had before so you're obviously ambitious and as you said you like a challenge. I was wondering what you see yourself doing in say five or ten years down the track?

Sandy: Oh ... that's a difficult question. Let me try to answer your question this way— I'm particularly interested in experimental design and also in teaching. I'd like to continue the organisation and planning side of research but do some teaching too. I know that you have lecturers here who do just that sort of thing—some practical work and some undergraduate and postgraduate teaching so that's what really I'd be aiming for—to be a lecturer here at the institute.

Richard: Well, that's certainly a career path that we'd encourage you to follow but of course it might be necessary to upgrade your present qualifications. I see from your c.v. that you've enrolled in an M.A. in Experimental Psychology. Could you tell me about the courses you're planning to take?

Speaker: Tape Exercise 8 (see Sample Task 5, page 109). Listen to the following radio news item. Fill in the gaps numbered 26 to 34 in the summary passage, by writing the missing words in the spaces below. First, read questions 26 to 34. Now answer questions 26 to 34.

Radio newsreader: Emergency in the State's Northern District. The Macquarie River has burst its banks, flooding the town of Stanton, about 300 kilometres north of the state capital. The Golden City and Macquarie Valley Highways—Stanton's only road links with the outside world—are totally impassable. This small wheat belt town with a population of about 3000 is now entirely dependent for its survival on the efforts of the army's Disaster Intervention Squad which is bringing emergency medical supplies and food into the area by helicopter. Our correspondent Maxine Zenith flew into Stanton with the army. Maxine?

Reporter: Well, Doug, conditions are really very bad indeed here. When the river burst its banks, it came with virtually no warning. As you can imagine, it's difficult to get precise figures about casualties but we believe that at least six people have been drowned and up to forty others are still missing. Local resident Mrs Mary Olsberg, who's with me now, had an incredible escape. What happened, Mrs Olsberg?

Mrs Olsberg: I was just in my car when this wall of water came shooting down the road without any warning. Luckily I was near the top of South Hill so I escaped the worst of it but the two people in the car in front of me—they were just swept away. The water came from nowhere. It was awful, really awful. One minute they were there and the next minute they were gone.

Reporter: The whole town centre is about three metres under water. Insurance companies estimate that about ten million dollars worth of damage has been caused to livestock and property. Virtually all the town's inhabitants have lost their homes and they're living in the tents which the army airlifted in. Commander Bill Pickering of the Army Engineers. What's the army doing exactly?

Commander Pickering: Well, apart from co-ordinating the rescue operation we've brought in five hundred tents as a temporary shelter against the elements. We've got a field hospital working. We've started evacuating the sick and elderly and the rest are, as I say, in tents at the moment up on higher ground. Obviously this is a temporary solution and we're planning to evacuate everybody as soon as possible. Weather conditions are still pretty bad and floodwaters will continue to rise for a few days but I would stress that there's no danger for those still remaining.

Radio newsreader: Commander Bill Pickering talking to Maxine Zenith at the Stanton floodings in the State's Northern District. Friends and relatives requiring information are advised to ring 668853—I'll repeat that, that's 668853. An emergency relief fund has been set up by the State Government and contributions can be made to the State Bank account number HK 51320. And now on to sport ...

Speaker: Tape Exercise 9 (see Task 17, page 112). Maya, a student at the Institute of Technology, attends a lecture on global warming and its effects on coastal areas. Decide which of the notes (A, B, C) contains all the main points of the lecture. First look at question 9.

We're going to look at the effects of global warming on a particular country to get this thing into context and I want to look at Australia, a country with 12,000 kilometres of coastline. There's a whole series of problems. What I mean by that is that in a country like this there are floods, droughts, cyclones, bushfires, landslides, earthquakes, soil degradation. You name it, we've got it.

OK. Now on your handouts there is a list of reading material which you should have a look at in preparation for your tutorials next week. I'd particularly recommend the *Greenhouse Effect* by Henderson-Sellers and Blong – they're very good on the Australian situation. For general background, Lovelock is good and the book edited by Pearman offers a nice review of greenhouse issues in Australia. I've put them in Special Reserve so you shouldn't have any trouble finding them.

OK, so I'm going to start today by looking at one of the most serious effects of a change in the global temperature—that is, a rise in sea-level and as I said I'm going to concentrate today on the effects this would have on the Australian context. If we assume that there'll be a metre or so rise in sea-level over say the next fifty years—but unfortunately the situation's not so clear because we've got to take into consideration a variety of scenarios such as increased precipitation at the poles which might actually cause a fall in sea-level. Anyway, taking this figure of a metre rise over, say, the next fifty or so years, what are we going to see? Well, we'll see an effect on flooding of structures on the coast —you know, houses, sea walls, ports and the whole infrastructure of road, rail, power lines and cables and so on.

Secondly, we're going to be seeing shoreline retreat in some low-lying areas. The sea will move inland in areas such as the Gulf of Carpentaria. To put it another way, in low-lying urban areas your nice beachfront apartment may just end up floating away and your parking lot two hundred metres from the beach will end up as prime waterfront estate. Most Australian cities are on the coast and in the case of Brisbane in particular—well, take a look at this overhead. That's roughly the area indicated by the blue line that's going to be affected with a one metre rise in sea-level. So if you're thinking of investing in real estate in this area, take my advice—don't! Again, though, it's difficult to predict the situation. Local conditions in some areas may actually increase the deposit of materials effecting an extension of the land. But whichever way you look at it there'll be a fairly radical change to many eco-systems and if you recall last week's lecture on change —well, we're really opening a can of worms here.

Apart from coastal flooding we should expect the penetration of salt water systems into estuaries, rivers and lagoons. If you think about the Myall Lakes system for example— well, the whole freshwater complex could be reunited with the sea. One of the most serious direct consequences of this for man of course would be seepage into the ground-water – in other words, the sea's salt water would enter the water table under the land. This would cause salinity in sources of drinking water and irrigation.

Thirdly, we should expect to see a rise in temporary flooding of coastal areas. I'm not talking about flooding as a result of increased rainfall, although that's another considera-tion I'll come to later. For now, I'm talking about flooding as a result of higher tides. Think about it, the swamping of the stormwater drainage system. What's that going to do to the street you're living in?

So, in summary, as we've seen you've got coastal flooding, destruction of coastal struc-tures, shoreline shifts and saltwater intrusion. I'll come back to some of these later but for now lets move on and look at tropical cyclones. Everyone remembers Tracy. Or maybe you don't because that is going back to 1974. I'm getting a bit old.

▶ ANSWER KEYS

▶ UNIT 1: READING

SAMPLE READING TASK 1

1. topic
2. impossible
3. assess
4. ability
5. strategies

SAMPLE READING TASK 2

B

SAMPLE READING TASK 3

C

SAMPLE READING TASK 4

1. multiple choice questions
2. gap-filling exercises
3. matching questions
4. open questions

SAMPLE READING TASK 5

B

TASK 2

Sample answers:

1. A newspaper article describing the increase in the number of science students, where the increase is occurring (schools, universities, the reasons for the increase, positive and negative effects).

2. A newspaper article describing the recent level of exposure of political candidates on television, the role of the media in the political process, possible solutions and problems.

3. Part of an essay describing and restating the major points, making recommendations, drawing conclusions.

4. A chapter in an introductory textbook describing the basic principles of economics.

5. An article in a magazine or brochure describing the problems experienced by foreign students, such as the difficulties involved in coping with another culture/language, and strategies for dealing with these problems.

6. A manual for prospective overseas students describing the things they need to know and do, such as obtaining a visa, getting language assistance, preparing for their courses, knowing where to find help.

7. A short, concise outline of a thesis or journal article describing the subject and main points of the thesis or article.

8. A magazine or newspaper article describing the increasing importance of the economies of the Asian-Pacific region, the history of their development, and their potential impact on the world economy.

9. A magazine or newspaper article arguing that immigration is beneficial to the economy, giving examples of the benefits.

10. A magazine or newspaper article describing the conflict between large corporations (or countries) which produce and use hi-tech products, and discussing the effects this might have.

11. A set of instructions describing how to use and look after a compact disc player.

12. A list of things that students must and must not do at college.

TASK 5

1. Oceanographic surveys ... every ocean.

2. In conclusion, the report ... on the economy.

3. Endemic goitre ... an iodine-deficient diet.

4. Definite hypertension ... rural populations.

TASK 7

A. Time – (after)

B. Cause and effect- (As a result)

C. General and particular

D. Contrast/comparison – (on the other hand)

E. Addition – (Firstly; Secondly)

F. Time – (In the 1940s; In the 1960s); Cause and effect – (Hence; Led to)

G. General and particular

11. Contrast/comparison – (on the other hand)

TASK 7

A.

TASK 12

1. F

2. T

3. N

4. F

5. N

TASK 13

Sample answer:

table of contents

preface

introduction

Unit 1

Unit 2

conclusion

appendix

bibliography

index

TASK 14

Problem 1	B
Problem 2	C
Solution to problem 1	A
Solution to problem 2	E

TASK 15

First argument 'for'	H
Second argument 'for'	C
First argument 'against'	F
Second argument 'against'	A
Conclusion	B

TASK 16

Stage 1   C

Stage 2   E

Stage 3   B

Stage 4   A

TASK 17

F, C, B, A, E, D.

TASK 18

they = notes

them = notes

them = notes

this = try to write down everything in a lecture

it = this (try to write down everything in a lecture)

they = some students

TASK 20

1. 80 students.

2. No.

3. The units in law ... government and education.

4. BUSL 300, BUSL 301 and BUSL 320.

5. BUSL 210 Foundation in Legal Studies; BUSL 213 The Legal System; BUSL 212 The Civil Justice System; BUSL 250 Basic Business Law; BUSL 300 Law of Business.

6. The great majority of students.

7. 3 credit points

TASK 21

1. allocation, distribution, stability and growth.

2. industry, commerce, banking, education and government service.

3. accounting, finance, statistics, politics, geography, law or sociology.

4. No.

5. Entry to these units will be guaranteed only to those students who have entered Macquarie under the Bachelor of Arts (Economics) quota or to students or to students whose entry qualifications were above those required for entry under these quotas.

TASK 22

C

TASK 24

The passage supports the statement.

Full-time study is extremely demanding requiring a commitment of perhaps 50 or more hours per week.

'Full-time study' = Full-time students

'requiring a commitment of perhaps' = may have to study

'50 or more hours per week' = more than 50 hours a week

TASK 25

1. A	5. A
2. B	6. B
3. B	7. A
4. B	8. B

TASK 26

Sample answers:

1. alter, abandon, adapt
2. liver, brain, kidneys
3. hiccups
4. evict, remove, sue

TASK 27

1. short-sightedness
2. a small tunnel used for accessing underground cavities
3. weight divided by height squared
4. hereditary chief

TASK 28

Sample answers:

1. drought, lack of rain
2. people who do not belong to the clergy (lay people)
3. married women
4. control, censorship

TASK 29

Sample answers:

1. speed, fatigue, alcohol
2. veto
3. analogue
4. rabies

TASK 30

Sample answers:

1. inaccurate, controversial
2. recipients
3. touch, handle
4. skidded, went out of control

▶ UNIT 2: WRITING

TASK 2

1. academic success in high school students
2. Listening challenges overseas students face in tertiary education/ recommendations

3. the use of chemical preservatives in food processing

4. study abroad/advice to a prospective student

5. the laws which prohibit the sale and consumption of heroin

6. benefits and risks of TV for young children

TASK 3

1. How do wage increases contribute to inflation?

2. How is crude oil refined into petrol?

3. What are the benefits and risks associated with tropical logging?

4. What are the factors which are related to anxiety in high school students?

5. What kind of listening challenges do overseas students face in tertiary education? What recommendations would you offer?

6. Do the advantages derived from the use of chemical additives in food processing outweigh the disadvantages?

TASK 4

1. Should (the laws which prohibit the sale and consumption of heroin) be applied to tobacco?

2. In your opinion should the government intervene in (the rights of the individual with regard to family planning?)

3. What are the effects of (the unrestricted use of private cars in urban areas?) What (recommendations) would you make (to improve the current situation?)

4. To what extent has (the diet of Melanesians) changed in the past 20 years? What effects has this had on (their patterns of mortality?)

5. In what circumstances can (capital punishment) be justified?

TASK 5

1. Has the traditional male role changed in the past 20 years?

2. Are coronary diseases preventable?

3. Is diet a contributory factor in stomach and bowel tumours?

4. Are the risks involved in genetic engineering acceptable?

5. Will migration from the developing world to the developed world become a social and political issue in the 21st century?

6. Should the decision to suspend a life support system rest with a doctor?

TASK 6

1. Has nuclear deterrence saved the world from war?

2. Is the dominance of black people in US sport due to sociological rather than physiological factors?

3. How have relative costs created terraced farming in Japan and extensive farming in Canada?

4. Why do climatic conditions resist prediction?

TASK 8

1. *Sample Answer*:
Over the last 60 years there have been major changes in the relative size of the major employment sectors in the British economy. In 1932, 25% of people between the ages of 16 and 65 were unemployed. Of those who had a job the largest percentage worked in the industrial sector, followed by those in the services sector and in agriculture and fishing. Only 3% of the population were employed by the government.

As the diagram indicates, by 1992 major changes had taken place in the occupations of the working population. Most significantly perhaps, a far lower percentage of people of working age were unemployed. The relative size of different occupational sectors had also changed significantly. The industrial sector only accounted for 15% of workers while the largest employment sector was made up by workers in the service industry. Agriculture and fishing had also declined whereas the government sector had increased enormously, employing almost 15% of all workers.

2. *Sample Answer*:
The number of people employed in the Australian mining industry has declined throughout this century. At the beginning of the century more than 60,000 people were employed in this sector but by the end of the first world war this had fallen to only 40,000. The number of employees continued to decline throughout the 1920s until the late 1930s but at a much lower rate than previously. During the second world war and in the years immediately following, the downward trend was reversed and employment grew to 50,000. However, from 1950 onwards the decline began again and was marked by a sharp drop at the beginning of the 1960s after which the rate of decline slowed. By 1990 only 15,000 people were employed in this sector.

TASK 9

Sample answer:
The computer saves time by working faster than the human brain and hand; it is an important educational tool; it provides information for practical and educational purposes; through the internet it can link people around the world.

Possible disadvantages of the computer include: invasion of privacy; the elimination of many kinds of jobs; the uncontrolled distribution of violent or pornographic materials.

TASK 10

Sample answers:

1. Providing various common sense rules are adopted cars should not be banned from city centres.

2. In this essay I will argue that voluntary euthanasia represents a major threat to the individual and should certainly not be legalised

TASK 12

Sample answers:

The need to train young people for employment should influence the curriculum of universities.

In addition, universities should contribute to the national economy by carrying out research which assists industry and commerce.

Society, however, has many needs which are not of direct economic importance.

Moreover, the goal of a university curriculum should be to teach people how to think.

Finally, because employment needs are constantly changing, it is important to have an educated rather than a trained workforce.

TASK 13

Sample answer:

Finding accommodation in Britain can create difficulties for foreign students.

Single or double rooms on campus are the cheapest and most convenient type of accommodation available to students. The demand for this kind of accommodation, however, means that it is difficult to obtain and many students therefore find accommodation in the private rental sector.

Finding accommodation in the private sector also involves difficulty. Although a wide range of accommodation types is available, rents may be high. Even when students share a flat, they may have to pay around £60 a week.

TASK 15

Sample answers:

Passengers should check the location of life jackets.

Hand luggage should not be left in the aisles.

Cigarettes must be extinguished.

You should place the oxygen mask over your mouth and nose.

Shoes should be removed.

You should place your head on your knees.

You should place your hands over your head.

Passengers should wait for instructions.

TASK 16

Sample answer:

Refuse sorting involves two major processes: separation and collection.

Waste of various kinds, including for example glass, food and rubber, is placed on a conveyor belt which first passes through a shredder before moving to a primary air classifier.

This classifier removes shredded paper and plastic and deposits them in a compactor.

The remaining materials pass through a magnetic separator, which separates out steel cans and iron and deposits them in a collector.

Materials such as glass, food and non-ferrous metals are unable to pass through a trommel screen and are placed in a collector.

Residual waste which passes through the trommel screen is then removed from the conveyor belt by a secondary air classifier.

At this stage all materials have been sorted and are ready for recycling.

TASK 17

Version 1 has a clear introductory sentence, presenting the reader with an overview of the two essential stages. The two stages are then each described in the following paragraphs.

Version 2 includes the same information, but it is more difficult for the reader to follow because it does not include an introduction and the information is not divided into paragraphs which indicate the essential stages.

TASK 18

B and C.

B makes a recommendation about reducing the pollution of the sea, and C deals with waste disposal. Both are irrelevant to the topic of air pollution

TASK 19

Version 1 describes the functions of word-processing packages. It does not evaluate the effectiveness of these packages in teaching children to write. The information does not answer the question. Version 2 describes how word-processing packages can motivate children to write and provides evidence of their effectiveness.

TASK 20

Version 2 fails to answer the question. It discusses the general issue of heredity versus environment in the development of psychological characteristics but does not describe the techniques for determining the relative importance of either factor. Version 2 is a good answer for the question: 'Are psychological characteristics inherited or acquired?' It does not, however, answer the question asked. It is therefore irrelevant and would receive a low mark.

TASK 24

Essay A: In general this is a very poor essay. Although the main point is stated in the introduction and the conclusion the writer does not discuss any of the disadvantages of computer use. The argument is very unbalanced and badly developed. The examples are insufficiently developed, a problem reflected in the fact that the essay is far too short, only 120 words long. Additionally, the vocabulary and sentence structure are also very poor. It is often difficult to understand what the writer means. The range of structures is limited and very inaccurate. Spelling mistakes also make it more difficult to read.

Essay B: In terms of ideas and organisation Essay B generally answers the question satisfactorily although it is a little under the minimum word limit. The lack of length means that some of the ideas are insufficiently detailed; the discussion of the disadvantages, for example, is too compressed. Also, a result of inappropriate vocabulary and grammatical error the conclusion is hard to understand and undermines the communicative quality of the essay. In general sentence structure is reasonably accurate but the range of structures is very limited, suggesting the writer's inability to use more complex sentences.

Essay C: This essay is well structured, with a clear introduction and a well organised discussion of both the advantages and disadvantages of computer use. The argument is relatively easy to follow and contains a conclusion which clearly states the writer's point of view. Sentence structure and vocabulary, though fairly complex, are, however, less controlled, and contain inaccuracies which detract from the overall effect of the essay.

▶ DIAGNOSTIC TESTS

TEST 1: Grammar

1. c	10. b	19. c	28. a
2. d	11. b	20. d	29. c
3. b	12. d	21. a	30. a
4. a	13. b	22. c	31. b
5. c	14. a	23. d	32. c
6. a	15. c	24. a	33. d
7. c	16. c	25. a	34. a
8. c	17. a	26. b	35. b
9. d	18. b	27. c	

TEST 2: Sentence Construction

Sample answers:

1. Although the results of the experiment were successful, the government cut the funding.
2. She chose to study accounting because of the good employment prospects.
3. The tree guard concentrates precipitation around the root system as well as protecting against animal foraging.
4. In-vitro fertilisation has not only brought joy to childless couples but also created legal dilemmas.
5. The regulations concerning non-government schools, which were introduced in May this year, have failed to address the real issues.
6. As soon as the liquid helium reaches the decompression chamber it becomes a gas.
7. Enormous improvements in infrastructural development have resulted from breakthroughs in fibre-optic technology.
8. If she had not written so slowly, she would have finished the Writing section.
9. By denying workers compensation for industrial accidents, the 'fellow servant rule' effectively subsidised the industrial revolution.
10. As a result of the proliferation of the Crown of Thorns, a starfish which feeds on coral polyps, a significant diminution in the size of the coral reef occurred.

TEST 3: Spelling

supervisor	laboratory	inevitably	achievement
lecturer	parallel	predominantly	exceed
government	psychological	correlation	framework
section	concrete	material	progress
examination	criticism	discussion	chronological
proposal	pursuit	emphasise	modification
contrary	questionnaire	efficiency	distribution
opposite	comparative	variability	assignment
system	significant	review	separate
infer	sustainable	involvement	receive
analysis	equipment	consumption	observe
development	approaches	abundance	attempt
facilities	weakness	belief	perspective
appropriate	apparatus	theoretical	multiple
knowledge	approximately	graphic	estimate
responsibility	measurement	significance	parameter
resource	decrease	recognise	policy
experiment	sequential	maximise	response
characterise	elementary	summarise	pattern
gradually	simultaneous	synthesise	acquire

TASK 2

Sample answers:

1. Destination, departure and return times, days, dates, cost, need to sign up, things to bring.

2. Recommended reading, assignments, main points, examples.

3. Opening hours, cataloguing system, physical arrangement of library, borrowing rights.

4. Location and time of accident, name of ship, extent of oil spill, number of injuries reason for accident.

5. Rent required, amount of deposit, location of flat, distance from transport and shops, size of flat, length of lease available.

TASK 3

'Is Michael going by bus/by train/by taxi/on foot?' Anticipate words like 'walk', 'cab (taxi)'.

TASK 4

1. A
2. C
3. D

TASK 5

'What's your address?'; 'Could you give me your address please?'; 'Where do you live?'; 'Whereabouts do you live?'

TASK 6

4. Gerharde Esterhazy
5. 7.12.55
6. 13 Albion St.
7. 567 4990

TASK 7

890
15,640
33
234,980
1,435,756
742
387,313
569,030
781,953

54,278
63,726,867
99.21563
84.034
⅝
⁶⁄₁₀
23.3
34.3
89.074
12 ½
99.9
$1500
£99.90
$2500
$13.33
$30.13
£27.14
1965
April 20
1982
May 15
1799
August 2 1
1804
1939
September 8
1968
889 9745
919 5392
465 6578
02 891 653
987 344
608 6662
008 750 11 65

TASK 8

AAI
QKY
WUTT
HJP
JGE
BYI
AEH
RVG
EEB
IIE

BVD
PBD
SCE
RKO
IVT

TASK 9

Campbell
George
Christopher
Irene
Marco
Victoria
Hennessy
Winton
Cyril
Adelaide
Costello
Jerot
Glenda
Sitompul
Manchester
Ontario
Zoe
Leeds
Queensland
Harry

TASK 10

Sample answers:
11. Students require a <u>separate</u> library borrowing card.
12. <u>In term time</u> the Overseas Student Office is <u>open until 6 p.m</u>.
13. The bank is <u>open on Sundays</u>.
14. Students <u>can sometimes</u> cash cheques at the <u>Overseas Student Office</u>.
15. The doctor sees patients <u>only between Monday and Friday</u>.
16. If you want to use the gymnasium you <u>must</u> have a <u>special membership card</u>.

TASK 11

8.	T	13.	F
9.	T	14.	T
10.	T	15.	F
11.	T	16.	F
12.	F		

TASK 12

Sample answers:
22. Why did she apply for this job? (What was the reason? how come?) Sandy's

response: interesting, better salary, more challenging

23. How did she find out about the vacancy? (job/post/position). Sandy's response: newspaper, friend
24. Where did she learn to type? (study typing/learn keyboard skills). Sandy's response: taught herself, high school, secretarial college
25. What are her long-term goals? (What do you want to do in the future?/What are your aims?). Sandy's response: more responsibility/ higher position

TASK 13

Sample answers:
17. to understand people
18. the practical orientation of the course
19. researcher
20. statistical analysis
21. not challenging
22. to combine management and research/ she needed a challenge
23. from a friend (John Pincher)
24. on a secretarial course
25. to become a lecturer at the Institute.

TASK 14

Sample answers:
30. homes, offices, vehicles
31. homes, property
32. tents, huts, barracks
33. a telephone number
34. a bank account number

TASK 15

Sample answers:
26. burst
27. road
28. 3000
29. food
30. car
31. homes
32. tents
33. 668853
34. HK 51320

TASK 16

what I mean by that is ... : restating information in different ways

to put it another way ... : restating information in different ways

so what we've got so far is ... : making a summary

I'm going to kick off by talking about ... : introducing a new topic

what you've got to realise is ... : emphasising a main point

that reminds me of the time my husband and I ... : giving irrelevant information the crux of the matter is ... : emphasising a main point

as we've seen today ... : making a summary

in other words ... : restating information in different ways

this is not always the case ... : contrasting

the next thing we'll be looking at ... : introducing a new topic

there are three main concepts you should bear in mind ... : emphasising a main point/ making a summary

however, you've got to remember ... : contrasting

TASK 17

A

UNIT 4: SPEAKING

TASK 2

Sample answers:

They have already studied at high school:

- *What have you studied?*
- *Did you enjoy studying?*
- *What subjects did you find most interesting?*

They may have some work experience:

- *What sort of work have you done?*
- *Have you worked for long?*
- *Do you enjoy working in this area?*

They have moved to or are planning to move to an English-speaking country:

- *How do you feel about moving to a new country?*
- *How have you prepared for moving to a new country?*

They may have a particular major field of study:

- *What did you specialise in at university?*
- *Why did you concentrate on that field of study?*

They come from a place that the interviewer probably has not been to or does not know well:

- *How do people spend their free time in your country?*
- *Could you tell me something about the food of your country?*

They are planning to enter tertiary or further education:

- *What do you intend to study?*
- *Do you think you will find the course difficult?*
- *What do you intend to do after you finish studying?*
- *Why did you choose to study in X (name of country)?*

They are not native-speakers of English:

- *Are you studying English at the moment?*
- *Are you interested in taking more English courses?*
- *What aspect of English do you find the most difficult?*

TASK 6

2. L

3. C, F

4. A, D

5. B, E

6. H

7. G

8. I

9. J

TASK 10

Sample answers:

When did you move from Rio de Janeiro? Why did you move? Do you prefer Brasilia or Rio de Janeiro? How do the two cities differ?

TASK 17

Sample answers:

2. When do flights leave?

3. How long does the flight last?

4. How many stop-overs are there on the way to Bogota?

5. How much does the ticket cost?

TASK 18

Sample answers:

Is there a television in the apartment?

Are there any schools near here?

Does the flat have air-conditioning?

Do I have to pay a deposit on the apartment?